The New World Written

The
New World
Written

Selected Poems

MARÍA BARANDA

TRANSLATED FROM THE SPANISH

EDITED BY PAUL HOOVER

YALE UNIVERSITY PRESS ■ NEW HAVEN AND LONDON

A MARGELLOS
WORLD REPUBLIC OF LETTERS BOOK

The Margellos World Republic of Letters is dedicated to making literary works from around the globe available in English through translation. It brings to the English-speaking world the work of leading poets, novelists, essayists, philosophers, and playwrights from Europe, Latin America, Africa, Asia, and the Middle East to stimulate international discourse and creative exchange.

Yale University Press books may be purchased in quantity for educational, business, or promotional use. For information, please email sales.press@yale.edu (U.S. office) or sales@yaleup.co.uk (U.K. office).

Set in Electra and Nobel types by Tseng Information Systems, Inc., Durham, North Carolina.
Printed in the United States of America.

Library of Congress Control Number: 2020951710
ISBN 978-0-300-24124-2 (hardcover : alk. paper)

A catalogue record for this book is available from the British Library.

This paper meets the requirements of ANSI/NISO Z39.48-1992 (Permanence of Paper).

10 9 8 7 6 5 4 3 2 1

CONTENTS

Paul Hoover

Born in Mexico City in 1962, María Baranda is one of the leading poets of Mexico. Her work has received Mexico's distinguished Efrain Huerta and Aguascalientes poetry prizes, as well as Spain's Francisco de Quevedo Prize for Ibero-American Poetry. Encouraged in her youth by the great Colombian poet and writer Álvaro Mutis, and later by Octavio Paz, she is known for her sweeping and incisive long poems and book-length projects, such as the sequence "Letters to Robinson." Of the volume *Ficticia*, in which the Robinson poems appear, Forrest Gander writes that María Baranda "keeps honing in on one of the most expressive lyricisms in contemporary Mexican poetry." He refers also to "her complex prosody—the pitch and tempo rising in plangent cadences that break into sharp, percussive counterpoint." The sea setting of *Ficticia* is in perfect keeping with Baranda's verbal momentum and fire. Despite their epic weight and size, her poems do not patiently narrate. Their way of telling is instead a stark announcement of being similar to an invocation; for instance, in *Narrar* (2001):

> A cry that in itself
> is the size of the sea
> and lives at the center of rapture
> and with each step it yields
> to the delirium of a sponge
> that inflates in sweat and gives glory

to the time of silent prayers
A cry is the caiman's vigil
the unleashed whip of an ant

For Baranda, narration is not of social relations but of the essential. Her cry is resoundingly of sea, sponge, ant, and prayer, as related in rapture. The poem's broad perspective may be influenced by the intensity and range of Vicente Huidobro's *Altazor*, an untranslatable word that joins "high" (*alta*) with "hawk" (*azor*):

I love my eyes and your eyes and eyes
Eyes with their own flash-point
Eyes that dance to the sound of an inner music
And open like a door onto a crime
And abandon their orbits and go off like bloodstained comets
    into chance
Eyes so sharp they leave wounds that are slow to heal
And can't be closed like an envelope

(trans. Eliot Weinberger)

Unlike Huidobro, Baranda does not introduce the "I" of herself as author. She richly embodies the other. The speaker, we know from the Góngora epigraph of *Narrar*, is "she." Therefore, the cry is that of a woman as well as the sky, a dolphin, and the caiman's vigil. The world does speak for itself, but as we know from Wallace Stevens' "The Idea of Order at Key West," it is a woman singing by the sea that "makes the sky acutest at its vanishing." The feminine "I" in *Arcadia* has a universal point of view that is dynamic and shifting, being flesh, word, and thought:

I was female given birth by the words of the body.
Body checked and continuous, body whole and without
    knowing.

Body surrounded by its subject: sunken. Body in the eye:
  imprinted.
Body sealed at the edge of cartilage,
Body of mine,
Body of whom

Despite the richness of her verbal weave, the mention of the baroque poet Góngora should not suggest that Baranda is *neobarroco* in her poetics. In the fierce literary politics of Mexico City, strongly impacted by the dominance of men, she stands as an independent figure. She is a poet of epic vision, who views the broader tapestry of fate, in which we might recognize "an agonizing smile / in the punctual / sweetness / of the one who is drowning." That vision ranges from "the newlywed God" (an impostor) to "the sharp bite of hunger / under the yoke of a sugar mill."

In his poem "Pavilion of Nothingness" ("El pabellón de la vacuidad"), José Lezama Lima, the influential Cuban poet and writer, uses a Japanese tokonoma, an alcove in traditional Japanese houses reserved for the display of art objects, to represent the imaginative power of emptiness waiting to be filled. In Baranda's work as in Lezama Lima's, many figures compete for metaphorical control of that emptiness. Characterized by layers and multiplicities, the work of both writers communicates the provisional and necessary. The provisional act of Lezama-Lima is to cut a crevice with his fingernail in the paper wall of the tokonoma. All is made possible in his poem, from kangaroos to sapodilla ice cream, by that one marking, analogous to the pen on paper. In Baranda's *Narrar*, a "maelstrom of all the whales in the sea" is invoked as such an absent presence. We speak of the "purely poetic," but the poetic includes the nearly empty shrine of possibility and the messy actuality of life. Baranda works toward the maximal and the simultaneous, where the motive is fate. The drama of her cadences in Spanish is not disguised by English translation. For a better understanding of *Narrar*, however, ask a Spanish speaker to read the first movement aloud: "al mar un grito / que se rompe y se repita / que se vacie / y al tiempo de la sal." The rhythm of enunciation is remarkable, especially when Baranda herself is the speaker.

In his preface to her 2006 volume, *If We Have Lost Our Oldest Tales*, Anthony Stanton notes María Baranda's special relationship with the long poem, which he calls "one of the great achievements of modern Western verse." Stanton specifically remarks on her connection to the long poems of Saint-John Perse, Vicente Huidobro, Sor Juana Inés de la Cruz, and José Gorostiza, author of *Muerte sin fin (Endless Death)*. Her proclivity for the long poem began with her first book, *El jardin de los encantamientos (The Garden of Enchantments)*, published in 1989.

In his essay "Death and Solitude in *Dylan y las ballenas* de María Baranda," the scholar Óscar González writes:

> Maria Baranda's writing adds to the tradition of the modern long poem not only for a textual amplitude, but also for the dialogue it establishes between the diverse and the equivalent, between fragmentation and unity, when dealing with such complex issues as death, time, loneliness and failure, from multiple perspectives that do not lose sight of the entire structure of the poem, which is not based on the equilibrium of the terms but on the tension between them. In *Dylan and the Whales*, a dizzying succession of spatial and temporal knots are visited, to be revised or abandoned by the lyric "I."[1]

Baranda's long poem *Nightmare Running on a Meadow of Absolute Light* is remarkable for its force of language, dreamlike power, and connection to the poetry of Sor Juana Inés de la Cruz, whose

1. Óscar González, *El poema extenso en México*, ed. H. Oliverio Arreola (Toluca: Universidad Autónoma del Estado de México, 2012), 33. Translated by Paul Hoover.

words, taken from "First Dream," are scattered through the later sections of Baranda's poem. Striking as always for the magical and essential, it concludes with the intense four-page coda "Víbora":

> And I said *viper* and saw myself unscrewed, cardial and
>   unique,
> carnivalesque and spoken, more vivid by means of the simple
> tree of language, first among the gestures of all that blood
>
> gone from my eyes toward a point of-what-other, with the root
> certainty of how-one-is-made at that time only
> when fear is inscribed among the folds of the skin.

The figure of the viper emerges in Baranda's poems as a totem of poetic capability. Its movement is peripheral and subtle until it strikes, when its power is deadly. Baranda's poetry is so much of earth, sea, and animal presence — in a sense, posthuman — that the superficial social life of, for instance, Eliot's Prufrock, seems alien and profane. She brings our vision down and in, toward the green altars of the grass. If at the social level, girls appear in poplin dresses, they tie their hair with "a string of water," an image of the uncanny. Moreover, their mothers have prepared "seaweed bridges / for their daughter's vulvas." To read the poetry of María Baranda is to be awakened by a living mythology, bright with darkness. She also has a wicked sense of humor. In *Atlántica and the Rustic*, images of the bull and labyrinth are dominant, but a sly satire on the masculine is also transpiring:

> My Friend urinates slowly in the larvary.
> The blood of mares infuses itself, raw, on the males.
> The view of the bull dominates its head. It is necessary.
> The world happens, it shakes, it disperses in a straight line.
> Liquid of life. The bare bull, its exquisite cavern.
> Black garlands under light softened by urine.

My Friend says: Life alone forms a labyrinth. We must choose
to look into the distance: the man-circle or the man-frog.

Baranda has published thirteen volumes of poetry. Her 2003 volume, *Dylan y las ballenas*, received her country's distinguished Aguascalientes National Poetry Prize, equivalent to the National Book Award in the United States. Her selected poetry, *El mar insuficiente (poesía 1989–2009)*, was published by UNAM (Universidad Nacional Autónoma de México in 2011. With David Huerta and Coral Bracho, she is a leading contemporary poet of Mexico and a noted figure of all of Latin America. A prized figure also of children's literature, in 2019 she received the Ibero-American Prize SM, the most distinguished such award in the Spanish-speaking world.

Her poetry has been translated into French, Lithuanian, German, Turkish, Chinese, and Italian. Her poetry books in English are *Ficticia*, translated by Joshua Edwards (Shearsman Books, 2010), *If We Have Lost Our Oldest Tales*, translated by Lorna Shaughnessy (Arlen House, 2006), and my own *Nightmare Running on a Meadow of Absolute Light* (Shearsman Books, 2017), which contains the entirety of the title poem and *Narrar*.

María Baranda is at her full strength as a poet and has been widely celebrated in the Spanish-speaking world for years. The power of her work now deserves major recognition by readers of English. As the critic José María Espinasa wrote in the introduction to *Arcadia*, "It is not easy to find poets like this in today's world and we must celebrate her presence among us."

The New World Written

From A Hive of Sea Birds

Translated by Mark Statman

THE BEACH

I

Here you are
about to leave
about to attend the meeting of fear
and its call of compassion through other veins
about to encounter that open land of truth
that has pushed you to the vertigo of all your dreams.
Here you are at the gate and you don't know how to open it.

Here with your almost fifty years filled with fog
and confusion like an image blurred with desire
with the thirst for every possibility
                                    at the insult of being and to be again
romping under the habits of the sky.

        Bats enter through the five senses
of your five fingers that sink between key and desire.
        Only darkness scrutinizes the dementia,
seeks the anger, the new fire or pardon that undresses
the softest skin of a trembling heart.
        Night opens its flow of pride
licks on the glass the slashed force,
the thunder in the distance
the nipple in the eye and the eye
in the weariness of a man and his dirty nostalgia.

You are about to leave
to open the old river of a new grave.
Outside the lights like broken witnesses
they break while the *ding dong* of a door
mournful cry of a sad supplicant
who slowly murmurs life between the veins.

II

The scorpions hide themselves in your shadow.
You cry out from behind that door
          shut up
          I can't bleed!

A hinge in a white burst for the thirsting eye,
a cardboard stage for your choking,
a woman who is opened in two by her jaws
a hopeless young fish
                    looks in through the glass
                    blindly moves and undulates
                    burning you in a breath.
All life enclosed frenzied
all dreams in silence
all the streets lead to the same life
and all into all a drought so clear
only your mother withers inside her skirt.
Definitive zones.
Shipwrecks that sink at night.
and transforming themselves into an atrocious point of
    gesture.
and the gesture
sinks enormous and impossible in memory.
                    Who are you behind that spit?

It's the dusk at the feast of the wreckage,
                    the last street

in the last hole

of the last house

where a stranger divides the swamp of fear

and its invincible sympathy for suicide.

Your youth has a vulture's age,

the open sore with its earthly reason,

the earth burning in its fallen and expectant night

like a dark design which says *life*

to say *death*. Your double looks at you

in an image of an excessive rooster

and young

in a day false and far from false tasks

as if still young.

The features of your thirst are a single irrevocable line

the point of a cursed heart

that perforated the wound,

the crack of a perennial sea

beside the rope that snared

the lone tyrant night

the lone and idiot night that confessed your blood.

Let's talk little by little, nothing is certain.

III

It's cold on the Malecón. Strange is the body
the maggots weighed in the sand
                    their natural stage open at the roots
                    licked by their tongues
                    scrutinized each day against death.
        Nothing that's here belongs to you.
You have lived under the furniture, behind the portraits,
next to the moth-holes, tricked by a saint
and you didn't know.
        You are the foolish uncle of verses,
old falcon among the parishioners,
rope tied to all reward in the syllogism of neighborhood
the apparition in ephemeral weariness of the women of that
    neighborhood.
        And you didn't know.
Everyone in a spiral of vice,
in the delicate memory of a nightmare made wet by your ether.
        And there was no blood. Only your dry veins
awaiting the new religion of theft,
the point exact like the pay for your crime.
        And you didn't know.
Nothing was worth more than that word and your passing
    pleasure,
your entry without a compass like a pin in scale-less skin:
        What were you looking for?
Now the street takes you to other obsessions,
                    rituals where faith crumbles
                    in markers made of coal.

IV

You want a new comb
to change what you think.
Skin won't reach the fire, the chorus
insists on vegetating under the dawn, gathering the frightened
palms at a boiling melting point.

It's night. Outside the wind tapping
against the dream-light wakes the appetite
of those who arrive at the bottom of absence.
There are those who open their skirts
the way they slowly open bottles in summer.
>   Only the vertical blood,
>   blood diluted in the syringe
>   sticks to the wall, sucks
>   the ration of time
>   sucks the newly to be in the world
>   with an arm extended
>   in the dying night body within,
>   whose language is irreparable in everything.
Your faith melts a little
in the window of the door.

You advance wet and dead by the stone.
You say the new flowers, the gravestones
of air, what has and has no importance,
is yours. You watch over the language of the guilty,
you paint the entrance to the cave sky blue,

what resists in praise and then multiplies
is another prayer, another voice, another perimeter.
The age of each deciphers your argument.

You see transparent tides in a country
where the key to pardon is but an earthly method.
There they call it Calamity
        Survival
        Mutable time
while a girl goes whistling in these lines.
Her eyes speak in the dark, they condemn her innocence
with your name that enters and leaves through her ears.
And not the lightning
and the mouth
not the mouth
and the lightning
persuade her to join the first cry,
the first moment
warm and flushed
in the mental grave of your words:
        Come on, come on so that love is inside the mouth.
You'd like to dig up her lips
but you can't even open the door.

Your mask one of panic.

V

Your father has used your shoes
and your father has dressed as a lover.
The lips of rain are invisible gold next to the rod.
The rod where the dry thirst of the wake accumulates.
The invulnerable church in its orthodoxy
has domes of lightning,

> crystals with rams
> barefoot musicians
> bodies of saints flooded by fever.

The pews guard the emptiness of the oldest pastor.
They seem trunks frayed by the salt of promises,
other promises
when the children sing astonishment
the life beneath the blessing of a psalm.

The voice shortened into sadness
under the amber of a woman with child.

Horses of illusion fill the Plaza.
Meanings of an interior being falling to pieces.
Your hand reaches to look for crumbs on the table.
Flares of a world that ends

> and there, in front of your island,

rolls the heart of a man
awakened in the shoes of a stranger.

VI

Lachesis gives herself over to the pleasures of a deer.
Bad news. Sweating glass. Serenely taking comfort in
        the edge of dreams.
Her red mouth, a cry in a purple well
        of lips half-open.
The shaking fear of her skin.

Thetis saves a bloated fish by the shore.
        She pulls chairs to the edge of blood
        and speaks of the dead as if they were
        still alive and barking for their view.

Everyone has gone, says Mary.
        They've been murdered with bullets
with their faces of sun alone in the vineyard.
They bark their names.

If one time they run as if they were birds
        in emptiness, stupidity in emptiness,
        we will all fall,
        says Argo in smoke at the bottom forever
        with his broken sandals in the cold mud.

Zeus traces in blood the image of a viper.
        It licks with joy, flicks its cleft tongue
        to the scabs under the line of its lips.

Everything burns me,
      Lysistrata complains.
To the foam of my tits like
a silent flame of lightning.

Homer shakes dust.
He thinks in dust.
He illuminates dust like a brilliant fish on a ladder.
His eyes are the shock of blood
that each bone sinks,
each bone that burns under the candles of deepest joy.

VII

The beings that I am break into pieces.
They embalm their organs with *aguardiente*
and a rag marinated by the open sky.
Vocabularies in plain desperation.
Words fallen from their hands
licked by street dogs.
No one understands me. I have decided to scrutinize
the limbs of other prayers, folded
in the matter of oblivion.

      Animals and maggots
      sweet imaginings of someone I was
      someone possible, an almost reflection
      in the kerosene lamp.

Thousands of roaches run by me. Fire in my hands.

      I walked watching the sea with men
and I saw inside their eyes

      a forest of birches at the side of the shadow
where a flying bat, silver blue
cried in the half-light of a bird's heart.

      It was the time of hunger on the island of red fish,
in the gardens of ablution and fortune.

      It was the time of the stone
when the afternoon named itself with a blow
between the wings of birds and, on all the postcards,
a Christ on his knees fell face down.

      It was time, simply,
and I saw pass ancient gods working

in the vegetable garden
next to the old tongues of men.
        It was a fog then
        and I
        was scared of the men.

VIII

Fear. Fear of not being, and to not be
where one can be one or several things at a time
(the consciousness of *being* always falls to pieces):
I am no one
      and I gallop in the slow water of its oceans,
I am father
      and I squeeze fresh oranges like the air,
I am a fly
      and I die every day like soft flesh
      while standing I grow older before the dishes.
The vegetable sellers pass, the riders from the stables,
rodents that admire the fresh fruit of their temples.
They pass with their white gowns and their black stains
of dried blood, of clouds full of their songs
in the jaws of time and their ropes
for killing the cattle in a celestial candy store.
They pass while I dream
of a rotted island ahead of their dreams,
of sweating watercress, of solid rains that seek
the face of death.
      Outside an angel licks the shoes
      of fierce poisonous women
      in the green river of red snakes.
He asks them to let him fuck
with a pair of shoelaces ahead of his fever.

I have every face of the abyss.
Flashes of lightning seek me with their bolts.
It's the arrogant order under the eyelids of wind.
Skeletons dressed with the grace
of one who loves a girl
where there was no God to drink their waters.

Hills above my sky.
Let no one strip me naked!
Let no one remove the light from my knife of gold.
Solitudes of a bone crushed in the window,
spoons for eating like a one-eyed soldier fireflies at dawn.
The birds pass with the tattered sun of winter
burned by the blood of terror.

For whom do they wait?

IX

A slow animal inhabits my entrails,
its cavernous skull a hole of light
from where it looks out on the world. Its greedy mouth,
its absurd walk, its treaty with my bones,
it is an avalanche the crying of wind and darkness.

Sometimes the crashing sea stops on my forehead,
makes me feel the rain on the prairie,
the forgiving doubt of a night
converted to mud.

The days and hours grow in me,
deep inside this austere animal,
small god of misery,
soliloquy of a sick shadow.
I am like this when the frogs sing
and the dogs bark in my heart
and its refuge of coal and mud.

I have a reason to scratch my belly,
to drink the years of adulthood among the birds.
It's necessary to attract a hungry port
of the imagination joined to the impenetrable shadow
of a crime. There, where no one knows,
where only the light of that imagination
so respectable exists. It's necessary every moment
as if it were a horse
that runs through the valleys at the speed of song.

Infallible song joined to a matting of clouds,
clouds in a port devoured by birds.

I live thousands of miles from others
people without peace or words, lovers of wine
and the foam where the festivals of coal
burn between the circles of smoke.
I live joined to the improbable talisman
of a mistaken reason,
an illuminated wood from which the songs leave,
joined to the bird of good, birds
that leave my dreams
when I peed by the birch trees
in the last small corner of the night.

I know dry faces of invisible men,
heroes of fiction, of truth
and the horizon, men distinctly new
more servile now and more uncertain
I watch them with horror, I hear them walk
between the wands and caverns,
fall the way in a fable
a village without beauty falls.
They make me laugh those men that need
a hat as if they were a fish
shipwrecked in a storm.

Men, dizzied shadows of this earth,
joined to a shopping cart for candy.

X

Terrible heart lost in thought
you lose faith and fever in your excesses,
the hammer that every day is heard
striking at a point in the road
of children and crabs and birds.

Come here, come closer, don't look anymore at the stone
by the skull, the hard shadow
crumpled and cold in the sea
basin and the sunken joy of one who suffers.
Be quiet here, at the edge of the forest
where the birds recite
their long accumulated solitude, so that you,
terrible heart of chisels,
in this dry land can curse them.

Leave off that bread and the grace
that anoints you with devotion
first with that flower,
unexpected flower
that involuntarily
surrounds you under a neutral sky
of the senses,
with its tall stem of thorns
with your name and its unearthly
darkness of unexpected being.

Leave off, then, all that happens
when the joy of a distant age
is only one more cry
in the deep and blurred imagination of the vulture.

The vultures have made noises since the Apocalypse.
They slide in a bed of volcanoes
and ink, perhaps
to fill their lungs with blood
and like that they can cry with that voice at the edge
of the sea already torn apart
with their name.

The vultures are the gate for the dead,
the slow play of moss on rock
the tongue of a horse open on the prairie
in the dry and dense burning lime of dreams.

The vultures are
one more hope to ask of the moon
and a red road for the world
that graces a mistaken prairie.

The vultures joined to you are an instant
in the deaf song of another life.

From Nightmare Running on
a Meadow of Absolute Light

Translated by Paul Hoover

NIGHTMARE RUNNING ON A
MEADOW OF ABSOLUTE LIGHT

> *The world enlightened and I awaken*
> —Sor Juana Inés de la Cruz

And nevertheless, here
almost
unsuspected, tired of seeing the voices
stripped from the land
—another earth, other lips of another cutting—
the modesty
of the flowers that torment, how much
brightness looms
at the edge of everything
and therefore
what's not known.
And I,
why didn't I know
of me?

Otherworldly, delirious,
unapproachable
at a point
pertaining to and named
pendulum
in the eye
uncorked: covered in dust: placed
removed
and
discarded.
It burns and declines
alone,
infinitely alone,
pounded, dismembered, broken
despised and deflated
it arises
in the shadows,
nightmare
running
on a meadow of absolute
light

. . . and when I ask myself
who could be persuaded
seeing that sonorous sky,
the open breach in the wall,
the movement in its measure
and the field in a fabric of herbs
sustained in its membranes,
alone, so alone, exhaling
a new punctuation, a long
cry in the aggravated night,
forced to see
a glimmer of what was,
telling yourself the same:
bad, worse, ill-fated,
and I think about this disproportion
of thought,
in the astonishment before a pause,
a compass stopped
on a nonexistent phone or on a CD
timorous and solicitous, a *now*
in its intent to be flame
between even darker lips
when the fish,
you said, were twice
speechless
always in the cavern
where the sun opens
disobediently

a defense
against the darkness
or a simple opaque
form
that you saw among atoms
and molecules,
dreamed?

You briefly switch on a galaxy and touch your childhood sea.
  The world is a dark road where night is the voice of what
  you say. At the sound of water you think of celestial birds,
  clouds, and a bit of sun in a story that begins without
  words.

. . . . because I look far away
fallen to the bottom, caught in the mud,
hidden in slow, solitary thickness,
because I say *fire*
and it rushes from my mouth
in flames,
because I name you now
as then
and the birds are more fragile and the clouds
no longer exist,
because I see you on the path of high stone
that imagines high meadows, diverse,
and the inhospitable matter
where articles
in the same reflection
that walks and talks and evaporates
and because everything is a page of hunger
where you reconcile the impossible
with only the single sun in syllables of the Advent,
because the night,
this night,
night virtreous and tiny
the most furious and insistent
which oxidizes itself as lightning
with this high form
has a putrid empire
with its eyes wide open, its field
of aromas in cages

its cry like a mean mule

that never forgets

—no—

and that it is there together with us

in order to die a little

from time to time and with the sleep

that is night,

that night

unique and pyramidal,

and completely yours.

The dogs of night break out of their dreams together. They
lose their eyes. You clarify reality with the laughter of the
waters. Then the world goes missing to ride on a single
wave like a lament in the burning arousal of cholera.

. . . and when I hear of the style
in which the wind howls over those old
flowery faces of clay, I think
of what this city reveals
and hastily burns
in my hands,
in that same history
corrupted,
where I gulp it down blindly
in dark streets of ink and iron
traced in the dust
that roars alone,
where I see it plainly
and I am soon ready
to take slow sips
among the rats
and garbage dumps
centuries ago where you sang
and I feel it, her crush
on you
in my throat
like a cry
and stings
in its orphanhood of mud
and presents itself and me
dislocated
while the dogs
lick saltpeter

from the dead walls
and roll tinplate cans
kicked by the laughter
of children.
Its rattle brings up in me
a flower of rapid water
in their drains
and leaves me
beneath scabby heaven
listening to its gravel
of *vegetative color*
its separate arms
extending
a dry cry, slow
in the repentance
of fire.

Toc-toc-toc, change your name. You appear like a woodpecker
in the evening. Nothing now remains. Outside, rocks
growl in the jaws of the fog. You'd like to be an alphabet
that spells the flight of the insect, a disappointment of the
relentless sun, with the high force of your instinct splitting
to pieces.

Light blindly, light
uncertain, light of mud,
light undulation of time
in the uproar of my fronds.
Light
of water, light incomplete,
light morally unfolded
uprooted pleading with your own
lips
don't let me
fall
into the heavens I don't know
stars to me
nearby
and deep in the dream
of the dream
that moans me and establishes what only I recognize.

It talks of clouds.
It precedes.
It shakes
and unveils.
It cries out to its mother,
icy wind
beneath the grass.
It's refractory.
In the shadows
it refrains
and consecrates.
Grouped
in their own language: it ceases.
And loves.

VÍBORA

I

And I said *viper* and saw myself unscrewed, cardial and
   unique,
carnivalesque and spoken, more vivid by means of the simple
tree of language, first among the gestures of all that blood

gone from my eyes toward a point of-what-other, with the
   root
certainty of how-one-is-made at that time only
when fear is inscribed among the folds of the skin.

And then, my flesh fixed in ink, congealed, I imagined
what I am, in that reality among the weeds
conceived in too much shade, too much hunger

hopelessly seeking the cry, my lips still pressed together
where it repeats and is exalted, wraps itself in yes,
always changing in nature in order to say: I am language.

I was language on another cracked scale and sweet
to place in the mouth, a pleasure of speech that shines:
I said *viper* and it was ample, opulent, a certain female bird

naked before heaven, fog turned into lips and said: again
to say *girl* in the animal's shadow, in the dark space
in that cry written where it's read in fullness: *poem.*

II

Blood in the vena cava. It can't endure its losses.
Venous blood in the anterior, speeding in droves
in that swallowing of one and another by an uncertain
    word . . .

or in that soft part where you drink the abandonment
of an idea that contains all of us, delays and
subjugates us before the silence of an indivisible figure:

the verb, the pure verb. The heart is quenched, defeats
maternal dreams beneath the crystalline fangs
like a dark and humid sun full of nothing and time. Time

that uncoagulates, spreading far beyond those wastelands,
uninhabited and muddled in the head. They drink, their lips
avid for other numbers, decantings, prophecies in water:

like a dense cloud you were created, baroque and resurgent,
your name fallen in the gallop of what's easier like insistence,
the repentance corrupted in your syntax. The ribs

generate gender and distance, are part of another idiom,
    threshold
of accents and syllables where this other innate anger arises
that shines a new fornication between your pages.

III

Poem of the world until it becomes unique, I survive
below the language in time, bulging and successful
together with achievements where, when mixed now

and if progress is made on mothers, faithless mothers
who speak in whispers and saliva, everything's more alive
between the limbs of a violated idea.

Distances masked by mossy gold, split
timber, the locks of so many dry heavens
clinging to that cloudy and written skin.

Until what you see is heard as a howl
(take it out) almost in the far (quickly), almost
desired (say it!) like a radiating happiness?

Whatever is not is only a breath in synthesis,
profane and spoken, thought in ether for a dead frog,
as if it were a plaster statue adjacent to such sites

and where everything is purified in the hollow consolation
of always between your segments of shadow being an animal
besieged by another animal here in the fear of my mouth.

IV

Suck me slowly, interlock your syllables and sing.
Sing me. Be my circle and abandonment. Idea.
Flash of the sun in my head. Golden in me,

focused and always true. Mythical gorgon,
sculpt your forked tongue along my curves
and enthrone all that's known that loves.

It spreads the love in your breath. It weeps.
Let me write without fear or panic,
that I am pulled beyond the longest branch

and listen to your first syntax, your dream
so amorous of a bullet interred in the mountain,
inflame me in the wind playing in my name

until you make me so pregnant, like a vast
and round idea, one that covers only me
and denounce the light already separated from the sphere.

Then I say: how much of the same blood
in my body, how great the mystery that breathes
in layers and layers of words: I write.

V

There are old children already touched by other vertigos.
Angels without mirrors, nobodies who seek the misery
of a song, the hunger for an unnecessary theory.

Nothing serves, all is known to die between the avid lines
of a first branching :::
I keep an ancestral child in my bed. She bites me.

Filaments between her eyes where in a gesture an invisible
river breathes. Only one. One like a slow whisper
that poisons. Now, its tongue cries for new paradises.

Extremes of a world where the dogs lose
their bone of night. It was night when we heard
the whispers of deaf men in the corridors.

Still, there is no poem. Everything's being placed on the bricks
among the nails of the dead. Songs next to the stone,
the button of fire of an authentic mex-mex. And that's it.

Everything pleases the anonymous palate. And there are no
    endings.
Only a breeze like a herald of the open mother, mother CD
mother poem, sexual novice, exiled viper, mine:

VI

Kill her, milk her, take out all the juice.
Don't let her slither into consciousness.
Suck her wind's light, drain it. Call her adverb,

verb, truncated syntax, ancient alphabet: foul-mouthed.
Lose it at the edge of her figure. Stop her.
Tell her there is no sap, nor juice, nor letter.

A cavern is her language, an open container.
Her thirst is the land. Her absence. Her heart is shadow,
shell, suture of the dry land. She has no ears,

but she listens, listens under the smooth stones
hidden next to a sexless pubis. Slit with neither hope
nor daughters, limb of moist gestures, the viper

is thought, hardened reason, hollow of a god
dark and bitter, fallible and porous, smooth talker,
mound on the flatland, father, father, I said *father*

I came to tell you what mother told me to tell you
then, everything is spoken when time falters,
it whistles in its drumroll and lodges in its throat.

Arcadia

Translated by Paul Hoover and
Aurelia Cortés Peyron

Also breaking the earth has the writing of sleep
—José Lezama Lima

I was earth.

I was street, dust, home.

I was the father and the son, the daughter and mother and
     time,

the praise and the shade and its long road of mothers.

I was my own and surrounded like fire, truthful, fecund in
     forgetfulness.

I was dying beneath the imperceptible light and an afternoon
     at the end of winter.

I was stain, I was dust, I was a grain of sand and the insect
     plastered to the glass.

I was quicksilver, fruition, simulacrum, circumstance, and
     vestige.

Vestige and dizziness in the nervation of a phrase,

In the cold placement of the word in the text,

I was text.

I was female given birth by the words of the body.

Body checked and continuous, body whole and without
     knowing.

Body surrounded by its subject: sunken. Body in the eye:
     imprinted.

Body sealed at the edge of cartilage,

body of mine,

body of whom,

blind body.
Body in the descent to hell
and in the apocryphal salt of paradise.

Body at three in the afternoon falling off my face, worn mask
in the syllables dripping, random and capitoline.
Immobile, yes,
in the corner: girl figured in the verb
in the running blood at the outskirts of something,
in the beginning of something, at the imperfect summit of the
    eye
and the eye placed in the hand, dry and awakened, the hand
    that turns
and unlocks the deaf circumstance,
the waiting for a beginning, a stealthy fable
in a very strange place.
All of eternity at three in the afternoon.
The world in a fixed point, at an exact minute,
in the corner revealed by the light of dreams.

Body of mine,
body of whom,
particle opening, footprint on each tiny pleat
of the school skirt, of the Pleiades, and its opening in the world,
in the South because of the smoke, in the North drawn on the
    face
of river beings, simple metamorphoses that pass a few
    millimeters
from myself, grasp and thread, scattered edge,

Mediterranean edge, edge in the eye that burns
and sweats salt and meat, the skin deferred in the corners
   of the text,
inwardly touching the structure of beams and friezes,
mechanical unions, amphorae where nearness always awaits
like a point in pity, a drop in the fountain.
Grape of mine, in my belly,
barely living.
A living in the eyes that its sea announces, its inner city river
linear and woven on the inside and in the cunning
of being, of being in a main square of hungry words.

Superior vein,
stored tissues and glands that wave
in the streets and nooks and crannies as a single solar matrix.
All of the avenues and their death-like whiteness,
Their whirlpool of similarities and differences,
of furious encounters blood to blood,
verb to verb through the interstices of skin and its
   catastrophes.

Predictions of the sun:
the hard dry land of the skin falling into its scales.
Hoarse bellows of that land that sinks,
cradled by waves, different waves.
False ceremonial.
Shameful promises of a daybreak that never arrives,
that doesn't exist,
that dissolves in the breath of an already lost pity.

Everything escapes:
from the blood of the tree stopped
in the middle of the dream to this small wall constructed
with the patience of a leaf, a different page
where the rain came to leave the wrong song,
the pallor of a phrase never spoken,
the breath searching for another exit.
And he, where was he?

Cities that fall from my mouth
like pieces of an invented map.
Shades that hide themselves behind other shades
in the profanity of the skin,
in the unthinkable part of silence.
Feelings discovered at the tip of a false harpoon,
of the wrong spear,
of an arrow that never hits the target
and forgets the route,
like the stevedore forgets his new bottle for the voyage,
the light that one day saw him sinking
in the judgment of a different sea.

Faces knotted together next to the peace of a window.
Exodus in a country that wheels another way,
with the code of a distance dissolved,
an impassible form in which the shadows are hidden,
the other clairvoyance of what one is not
and what is not held
not even on the shore of a forgotten song.

Figures that smile in the mist.
And a strong moan that is heard, invisible next to another
    abyss.

I was a cell. An essential part
that hands rub in the absence,
the beginning of whom,
with the weight of a new body,
a principle of being, a thirst in the eye
and in the eye the complete circumstance,
the bone marrow and its open roads,
its thousands of curved and rectilinear shapes
for the squandering of blood, the spillage in the hollow,
the hollow and its *however* of animal and cave,
The finger in my sex, the sex as a first substance.

All the hollows of the sea
and voracious animal roars,
an animal that moves though stopped in time,
in the new metamorphoses of an inner and vestal city.
City that comes to my back, back of lip beasts,
of a beast with the taste of heaven, of a *café con leche* for
    the boy
on the table of a dry breakfast.
Taste of the first milk, milk spilled
in the writing and its slow letters advancing
on the avenue of my body,
body of whom,
blind body

like a precise song,
a sound that roars in its fresh current,
in its obsessional and fatal strait
in its being a simple ferry
that carries people from one shore to another,
from a dream that anoints new roads, progress,
holes, contradictions, tiredness from fever,
strange substances, perhaps lies from what's not said,
the unwritten, the impossible.
A whole life without future, never arriving to whom.

Miniscule magnitudes,
limits imposed by ancient and momentary burdens,
physical conclusions and muscular pain,
civil, ferocious.
Solitary dogs in the streets inhabited by light and garbage.
Remnants of other lives.
Lives that carry their own fears,
stained and full of tobacco,
of dangerous substances and fine particles
where no one lives, sleeps, thinks,
if not in the salt on the eye. The eye and its life circumstances.
The eye and what was seen long ago in a fiction already
    written.
Words that mean other words,
lost in years and years where it's known there's no possibility
of a last thing, a final distance, a first frontier
of the heart and its sudden daggers. Life without a future.

Future that stinks like the leavings of Homer and his night
    house,
its laughter asphalt and itching skin,
vineyards that hide in a spot, an inner crack,
perhaps a pause in the air, in the serenity one seeks
to narrate another time,
a better time. Wind in the South.
Epidemic of sibilant esses that arises
from the essential veins, from those riverine temperatures
where the sea burns in the throat of whom?

Borders and boundaries in our mouths.
Hollows where the longing and its circumstance are not
    enshrined,
its fine-tuned sound of the bell, its plague of eternity,
and its terror for the children. Children cared for by me,
my open hands like a substitute for bliss.
Decompositions of lime and its gold rings,
its fragile commitment of the torrent.
Its having lived twenty or thirty years
with the same plate, the same inner glass.

Early mornings unfaithful to sleep,
to the first waking where a rose bush is trimmed
and a life full of children clamors, children in the words,
children of night and day that halt new flags
regions imprinted in the first desire and the last,
the one we always live next to the light of uncertainty.

Pyramid-like hordes.
Advent of what is not there or cannot happen,
like the elegies of Tibullus,
like the feast of Prospero on the island of death.
Reference frameworks,
theories of an inner, sedative light,
a bonfire of the world and its novels,
stories told out of other faces,
strange faces,
faces that we won't know,
made up by basements and prayers that consecrate
and stop the cry and its nearby lung
the howl of the Marmara and its glorious future,
its not arriving at the opposite island,
the oldest city in the world,
the continent stopped in the grape
and its descendants in the mirror.
Its being unable to name another page
or write a better story,
a poem like the key to the world.
A world in the cry,
in the most atrocious desperation,
with its name of love
delayed in the body as if it were a lower heaven.

Detonations.
Soft moaning of the field and its copper stars,
its rooster imperfectly crowing

in the dawn wounded by things unseen,
unspoken, undreamt of,
only felt or sensed
by a soft and incomprehensible instinct,
a desire to be bacteria, beginning,
animal within the animal of this world.

False bonds. Bodies bound in places
where the rain shines in nostalgia,
at the edge of dry battles. Things falling apart.
Amulets on the necks of a tempest written
like the inconstant sheet music of an open
and minute bird that ponders the smoothness of air,
the slow emergence of a morning thirst.
Complaints of thirst in the feet
and its fine traces in sand,
in the exile of some summoned letters
and the dark heart that resuscitates thunder.

Knots gathered at other boats keeping silence,
saying goodbye in improvised piers of sorrowful wood,
near a Martín Fierro who touches other hills,
who crosses with his robe the uncloaked party of customs
or the reverberating patience of someone gazing at a reserve.
Smiles that grunt at the growl of the wolf at the door.
Lacerations.
Time of a skin within another written skin.
Questions at the last committee of the night and their white
    atonement.

Slow hills where flies encircle the desperation
of a first story, a moment in the beginning of things,
of the weeds that the rain animates only to anoint the mask,
the face of a planted field where no one found the promise,
the hunger of a river with no scruples untied the bandages
by flowing.
Guards encrypted in the frequency of the unspoken,
the unwritten, that which produces a resentment of wind
in the humming of fire. Submerged bursts between lime
and something like saltpeter, overlapping a story
faded
and less audacious than oblivion.
Who sings?

My mouth wide open to a letter that doesn't arrive,
an anonymous word able to solve the memory moving
    forward,
the chance part of a cell.
Vast explorations of a microscope.
What is seen: small arborescences on the skin.
Physiologies.
Death rattles to sleep in the future,
where there is nothing and no one,
in a nonexistent time,
a new foundation of flesh,
a deserted road in a different city.
Strokes of the world, world in the pockets of the afternoon.
Afternoons that fall from the hand,
stones.

Fables under an exiled sun.
Tribulations for the voice of the public.
The sea, now, is a lance of fear.
Fear and its prophetic nails.
Its slow scratching that submerges all the pain
in a Sunday on the field.

Dry plains.
Disappeared houses in an impossible vegetation,
far from leprosy and the detachments of dream.
Visitations of a childhood in ruins,
in an apostasy that still tortures the calm of one who travels.

Virgins on an outlawed plain,
in the fine ligatures of a mystery
in the flashlight of a child
as if it were a time immobile,
a long stroke of uncertain light.

Households without names,
that hold in the white sweat of a handkerchief
the wall of misery and crying,
the possibility of concealing a kiss,
kiss and its path of fear
kiss and its taciturn walk in a story.

Honey in the wells,
fierce skies suspended in the dunes of the floor.
Forms where the fog anoints

the new atmosphere under other trees,
resentments of an unknown tropic
among those irresistible peaks,
artful stones dedicated
to sink the most intimate hands,
the most precocious wings
when the wind lifts.

All the world stopped at the corner of my thirteen years,
of the new world written on my skin.
Mouth open to so many internal cries,
to the new magma that runs through me
since that time like a black letter that advances, deaf
and punctual and true. All the world on the corner
of Insurgentes and Revolución, thousands of years and lives
    away,
of moments subtle and intimate, of time kept in the veins,
in the veins where the light flows
like the verbal essence of things,
the matter of the arm,
the matter of the dream
and the table and the chair that always wait for me,
as a vestal city is awaited. A city written
for me and lived by me,
a city is a fruit that explodes
like a desperate sun,
a speeding sun in my chest and my chest within my heart.
All at the tip of my tongue
at the tip of the look

of the edge that is seen and determines a form of life,
a being inside,
the very last of things and their profile of a rooster in the soul.

I was given my skin. Domes that open to other surfaces.
Sounds of stray birds with their wings closed,
with the light of a possible flame and its rosary of verbs.
Wet trains in a planned exile,
among sheets hung up for the green marriage
of an iguana with rain. Colors that petrify
the cries in different distances, in the vibration of a fallen
    word
as if it were the new key, the new password for incantation.

Salutations. Skin in my eyes and in my mouth.
Days without shadow over shadow days.
New sunsets inside the tongue
where a sea returns its alphabet of suns,
its other poems cancelled in the first salt,
in the foam dyed with false temperatures.
Nothing is channeled,
only the movement of the eye and the wedge that exalts its
    soul.

Cameras in the sky.
Hidden views that discover the reverse of history,
the recounting of what was gold and what could have been.
Silhouettes dismantled on a poorly polished table,
scratched by the emptiness of the dawn.

Pleasant meals on fortunate streets
where a letter moves and distills other laws,
the cold myth of a foreign woman in the Holy Land,
with the whinnying of sugar on her fine embroidered blouse.
Small pins on her tits,
in the brightness that migrated from her eyes to the dance
    floor
with the laughter of an outgoing heart.

Who was there?
The mother with the strength of a sea blowing toward the
    ember,
the daughter and her black mouth that split, the scream
of the victim in two and her coming disgrace,
the condemned woman asleep in the glare of another prayer
and the god fallen over its chair with its resin-soaked torch
    and its heartbeat
abandoned in the discord of the dish. Unutterable.
Dirty nostalgia scatters in a different land
where the door was closed at three in the afternoon.
But who was he looking at?
Secret landscapes wrapped in a brush of citrus,
a disturbing body that suddenly called for
the wings of a crow
and the fragile substance for the vanity of other magic.

Riders on the steppe. Raw bricks.
They spend the days between confusion and the exodus.
The sun illustrates a despairing god,

in the stench of the grass, a new form of opinion about art.
Arms fulfilling the lines, lightning that inhabits the intimate
    dullness of a nerve.
Absorptions that relax ventricular pressure
and the proximity of silence.

A dog barks next to a crab that has an old wound.
Medicine advances, the body regresses.
What is piety, is it an image of sense,
a port disoriented by climate,
a brochure of untranslatable lines,
where the guest holds its peace with a nod, secret.
The dog leaves, the crab dies.
Cold river mouths of skin and its opening,
ions that seep into the regions of sleep
before touching the cardinal cells
on an Atlas of blue and yellow.
Who speaks?

The mouth remains open.
The body leaves the body to gain altitude.
Streets of paper in the screeching of parrots.
Simple conversations
that deafen your cardiac capacity
a transfusion gone wrong
like a letter burning in the memory.
Lines extinguished for closed eyes,
scabs where the children were the other part of the night,
the previous exile in the body's suture. Everything gleams.

His name says that his hand is behind victory,
that false distance that still creaks like a sobbing of age,
of his god's pride ravaged in the whinnying of flesh,
a brief moment for other definitions.

Chimeras in the leaves of summer,
in the apocryphal part accustomed to the usual,
to shaking off the dirt from the cracks of the nail
in the memory of a palate,
that almost licks the fifty years,
the fifty steps that fold
near a charmed heart
the form of new advents
breathing in the shape of new advents,
scars tattooed on an old nopal.
Now, when the eyes are filled with fear
and smoke disperses the birds of air,
the breath is increasingly closer to earth,
and has the weight of an incomplete work
not approved by the fables of another place.

An insect plastered to the glass, to the configuration of being
and its memories.
Sad news. The South wind roars in the North.
Crustaceans on the tip of the tongue.
Remote seas that anoint their foam in new biographies.
Situations where the skin is embedded
in the shell of a bivalve
until it changes the soft sermon of its syllables.

It was in spring.
The leaves showed their fondness of earth in a precise
    language.
Everything was less dense when the voice,
with its offering of lime and fear, became thicker.
Walls gave way, the heart opened full force at a random
party at the entrance of the hive.
Slow apparitions of the bee and its desire,
its life vertiginous in the most delicate part of the leaf.
And there was no force to stop its flight,
the sting was approaching the pain of the beast
and its sadly wounded existence.

I was that intolerable mark,
the branching of the bedding, piety of the scorpion
and its slow circle of fire. I had in front of me
the usual garden of false delights
with its judgmental fence to ward off pests.
Suction at the edge opened the possibility of other threads,
roots scattered in the burning torture of the word.
All descent was to reach the language
that imagines and kicks the crucible of the larva. Beautiful
    traditions.
Everything was alien in the dust and profusion
of that city that began to adorn another belligerence
with feathers, the mordant surprise like a slice,
the cutting of each second and the seconds refused,
palpitating in its adjustment of echo and new silence.

Everything like a capillary wound and the congestion of its
    swelling organ
in the stream of its small ferments,
in the transformation of its streets,
its ramps of overliving, oversleeping, and overdying.
Another was time in the underlying verb and its different
    zones.

Zones of the soggy heart open to the fig tree
and its fresh fruits for the deepest consolation.
Zones that leave palms deposed at the border of a moment
as if it were a casual whistle announcing what is not always
and what is not here,
in the forge of language, at an imperfect time.

Corridors for the wolves,
A time of salt together with the children.

Someone walks among the ruins of a lost city
and in its sweet darkness determines the site,
the new sentence where oblivion explodes.
        Auscultations.
Fallen parts from a language of another territory,
in the open song of the flower in the morning
near the owl's feathers.
Green oscillations of the light before your eyes.
Descriptions.
It was easier to die than to leave time
in Homer's drinking cup.

We walked along a single street,
a sample of what was tormented,
murmuring other vertigos, a portion of the mercy
of the temples that fall off from us, inciting
the whiteness of the stones, their fragile fatigue
that is still sculpted in every erased face,
in each gust of an infinity that never begins.
Each side of life in a house, each separation
of the cry in the silversmithing of the slabs established
in other hollows, monuments without peace or testimony
in idiotic ceremonies to save the eye.

The eye and its atrocious reason, without a future.
Channels in the roots of a tree and there,
as if it were the scroll long looked for,
the precision of the Virgin and her reason for the world.
World in the eyes. World in hands and legs.
Legs open for the slow dilation that bleeds.

I'm talking about who I was.
The one who made the text her representation of life.
The one who one day saw the hard dunes of salt as a possible
scenario, immediate, like the edge of another reality,
where one writes and says the contrary, intangible,
curious, forgotten words, putrefying in that which I am not,
    that I was not,
and don't want to become. Being without movement.
But all of this is not an imaginary page, an invented thread
    of life

between ink and paper, between my eyes and what I see,
    fragile
words summoned at the table of no one, asylum of the thirsty
    animal
hidden in my lyrics, in each one of my written accents.
Tapping of the machine and its fine embroidery on paper.
Creatures that inhabit the possibility of something else,
of becoming one in the generous absence of the verb.
The night arrives. I sharpen my pencil, open my lips
for the total definitive burst until I lose myself,
fluent and bestial, releasing me, giving my invisible self
its past in stone and sad events, barely a touch,
a heartbeat in the body, a margin that exceeded
all the boundaries, the moist trail where I perceived the
    footprint
and its most intimate impulse, the substance tied
to other ailments, to the days and their slow minutes
of waiting and terror, to the dark stillness of a splintered home
with its index of mother of pearl, of stunning radiation in its
    grain,
its mark of dust and on its back, of a calm breeze
where there is nothing or no one, just the amazement of a
noli me tangere, the "don't touch me" of the botanist.
Fruit open to the desolation of day, to the taste
of the beloved earth and its notion of strength.

Foreign tastes. Breaths almost sour, almost true,
in a conversation over the phone.

The sun now shines at its appropriate distance,
in the torpor of other bodies that prosecute grace
and the ablution of those calling for a different life,
a place of peace in the ceremony of the dream.
Red guidelines between the veins,
homes invaded by gold and their old lady's amulet,
their long animal smile under a skirt and new promises.

Heartbeats where love branches out in a mirage
of fine words that burn like dry blood.
The force of the fist strikes the piety of those who live
and fortify a restless signal, a siege-time.
It extends in an extreme zone.
The face is the watchman. Marked by veins, the age remains,
the thicket that unfolds like a wind
around the house and its whistling, its communication of
    vertigo
that holds a new time. Distant dawns.

Sheets in the transparency of a muscle
and its sad appearance of life.
A face is always that crowd of words
framed by the drunkenness of death. And the day.
Serenity. Time that dwells on its haunches
and floats like a lost desire.
Exclamations that burn in the melody that invokes a blind
    man.
Blindness of what or whom.
Immemorial laughter about what was said at dawn.

Crossings.
Vessels where thirst is the announcement
of a happy and monotone time,
serenity looked for
like a beggar looks for a forest,
the celestial jungle without remorse
for the passing of a sad horse
in the glare of a heart that celebrates
a life without pauses, in slow chapters,
where there's no drunkenness or thunder.

Text spilled. Text in the body.
Bodies that open to the expansion of another time.
Situations where faith meets skin
and instills in its hollows,
in the ventral part of the dream,
its thirsty word throbbing in my thighs
awaiting an agreed-upon renunciation,
an ill-fated river to confine its gentle whisper
to tell it is there, it is always, it is arriving.
With its vast similitude drowning me,
wanting to invent me between its teeth and tongue,
at an arm's length from what was, of what will make us shred
ourselves in a slow combustion of what is possible.

I speak to say my eyes. Blurred
stripes in the flame delaying in my chest
from a language just beginning. To say again

ragged alphabets of salt in the bones. Suns
that burn on the other shore, much stubble,
suppurations. All of my body is text,
life that comes out openly in the spoken lines.

I name what I cannot reach,
what you have of me in my rough skin,
what I had of me in my rough skin
like a burning blade in the trials of the wind.
Nothing of what I loved functioned.
Not the crack that opened its lips to other harnesses,
not the ropes binding the Cyclops in the hidden gale, the
      privilege
of having kissed those hands in the hands of the theft,
the exact dimension of other
fervent and helpless arteries, where that portion of the sea
that was seduction and strength, place and home, flowed,
a life marked by the first apostasy of infancy.

How much gray stone remains in silence
with its muddy cloth and its fire that burns in the pores.
How much does time exceed
in its own dilapidated utopia
like mud in the depths of the word.
What I touched in the dawn
was the telling of a soft life,
sweet form of what is not recognized
where a language, distant and secluded, surrenders.

Once I had left the last line,
the place of invariable truth,
and its severe circumstance of belonging.
At other times like a chosen theater
newly founded in the sky of a tribe
and the sudden absence of its step. Something
was lost in the mirror where an emotion
saw itself trembling in the first blink and in the second
when the fish took another life in the splendor of water.

I tell thirst from my lips.
Time diluted at the limits of those who do not sing.
Time recovered in the notion of a verb,
a passing before what is said,
before the wait for the silent touch and its hand movements,
its flow over the body.
The body and its acknowledgments,
the recovered part in one stroke, a small notion
of what one is in a city populated by water.
All the subsoil of what is thought
is lived in a certain way,
it flows.

Restricted body
inhabited in the spikes of the silence,
constructions of ice and its fine prisms of ablution,
cathedrals of filigree and light where a stained glass points
    to the uncertain,

to what will never be there or could happen. Forms of
the blunt being, without the angle of a straight line.

The wrong body.
The wrong house and time lost and dry
open to other ends. The air is now
an absent air. I lose my complexion.
My arms remind me of a sea, servile
and grave, a bit of ink inside the pen.
Everything is doubt like the stillness of water.

Again the dog trots alongside the loneliness of my skin.
Soon he will die and the ants will make another
feast of him. Crosses in alignment.
Dark spots on the tablecloth.
The page is meaning, time broken,
like the scrapings of the tree.
Hunger escapes from my mouth,
animal that I am, pigsty of a failure.
There is no longer a challenge if my body is one with the
      night.

The wrong time for that girl standing in the wrong place,
on the broken corner of her broken years
like a cliff of illegible accents,
of channels open to the moment's determination
and its fissures of fear and illusion of powder,
to the simplest tie on the lower branch of that tree

where there is nothing to show but the simulation,
its open wonder in saying, in skin and its cartilage,
its open wonder in saying, in building
behind the tongue the new trap in the new world
against the day and its renewed strength.
Now who will give birth?

Retreat. Time falls from one hand to another
between the softness of tears.
Clean plains in the glands,
bodies in other bodies that fall apart from afar.
The air gnaws at the house with its black wings
and its apparition of a thousand fallen nights fallen on a
    thousand lips
and its feast of paradise and earth, its new announcement
    of truth,
its trot open to the uprooting, a starry passion
like the voice of the abyss, the voice that always turns
toward another reality, full and uncertain,
but manages to whip up its flame
as the most certain lamp in this world.
Who bleeds?

I want to touch the Marmara. Put my hand
into the depths, spell each of its letters
and have them drip from me like dark saliva.
I want to say its name over and over again,
open my mouth and suppurate the wound
that still fails to form itself like a light

in the window, barely shines, the furthest
from us at the break of day. Sea
in the night fed up with other rhetoric, pasture
where we had seen the hour and its patience of a maid,
the plenitude of the shore held by the hands,
the Centaur forced into the shape of the question,
to the testimony received horizontally in the body,
torn among exact veins
unique and violent, dying in loneliness and depth
like an invasion of written words.

Everything that I was remains bound in the glass
on the side of light and limited space, the exact flow of the
     instant,
rare and unheard of, that passes through the molecules
of the crystal. And from there, my hand or beyond me
like a phrase constructed in silence, my hand and its attempts
at being, its traces of unique creature of mine or beyond me
like a phrase built in silence, my hand that feels
what resists, what is stamped and seeps through,
what allows one to say: I am here and from here I love you
again and again like the minute exhumation of the wave.
Feeling, too, what conforms to the arrival, to the threshold
where the letters extend, electric, the saying
on the tongue, in the street of before, at the time of now.

All subscribed to the new interstices of skin,
to sentences incorporated in the neck or ankles,
to the pieces of paper fallen from my lips

open to thirst, to the language exuding, with a sweet tooth
and consecutive in the dried veins of glass.
My language that falls off and spills,
conceals itself and holds succulent the suture of dawn.
My tongue of fish unfolded in the heaven of the body,
seduced and uncontrollable, ventral
in the silence, in the *one, two, three, ready or not*
here I come, and the hiding place of horror,
avoiding sight, saying, and even listening,
places populated by sphincters and sounds,
by warm bodies remembered
at the edge of other fears, other
thoughts, other fallen imaginations
in other mirrors. All my survivor language
and casual, *moridora* and deceitful in the fiery zone,
in the part that embraces generously and emphatically.
Do you see it? It is stain and dust, grain and quicksilver,
the delight and the vestige, the likeness of whom
in the outskirts of nothing, in the beginning of no one,
in the inaccessible trembling of someone.

Drip-drip-drip. Comes the announcement: a city
is an open mouth, the thread that sutures the verb
inside the bodies. Everything penetrates.
From the clarity of a time gone, as if it were
a simple and accurate task, a membrane
to survive in the hollows, a drawing in the pores,
a going toward the shadow in order to cry: *hold me*

in only one place, *kiss me* to be able to speak
from the paper as if they were the genitals
of oblivion, the feet of new cartographies,
the seduced eyes in the ink and its pathways
evoked by the letter. I was text.

I am text and I die in the ears of silence
between the fingernails of an apocryphal line,
a rare line, a glass for drinking time,
that time written from before at a distance
that doesn't exist, that is not there, but made me
what there was. To come back. Come back to tell it all.
Come back to write from the crack.
Come back to multiplying myself,
extending myself on the streets and boulevards,
through leaves I invent in the honeysuckle,
in the mother of pearl of my being and its sea that is read
from me, dismemberedly, newly
in what is not there, and was not, never was: *Arcadia.*

From Ficticia

Translated by Joshua Edwards

XIII: LETTERS TO ROBINSON

I

We heard the heron at the end of July.
It had come to sing with a solitary quack
of oceanic time and an uncertain and speechless
dream of girls, the dry voice of wood and distance.
Dark secrets of goodness. False visions
beneath this soil. Alphabets that herald
the cleaner letters of abyss.
The lookout of sweat has arrived
like a verb's shadow.
Where we speak of domestic things,
shattered glass, mirrors for the faces
of who we never were,
always leaves us behind.
Now we see a thousand faces immersed
in mundane files
of loneliness and doubt,
records for the crystal ball of apparitions.
Subtle features that never changed
us into a precise feline print.
Time dragged along
by the salt of a world
that never belonged to us.
Now that we rest our delirium
beneath a whitewashed sky we can desecrate
the secrets held by men of a never-ending

history: destiny's
small disciples. Women in the midst of absence,
places distinguished by a lack of rain,
liquors for the insomnia of those who didn't die.

Now that the light has been put out like a trace
of initial infancy, a lone crack
in our lives, we can travel with a lost bird's
invitation, with the winged idea
we once believed it ignited.

Now nothing is in the face of the wind: not the tinted verb
of familiar adolescence, nor that childhood
guarded by the beast in its jars of alcohol and prophecy.
Nor that adolescence of the princes of Eden,
kings of a paradise within an inescapable hole.

Now we can lick our trophies, the exact division
of a mask-filled forest that made us
into soldiers for a story without end or beginning.

II

Robinson you failed. Your mind was changed
into a vain mirage of disenchantments.
I'll no longer look after your home, that small den
where rain could undo the sink
of proverbs and relics.
I'll no longer look over your cave of salt and bread

where the scorpion's peace
is your measured anger's kingdom.
You will remain as stubborn as a shark waiting
for small prey. I'll watch you with doubt,
not knowing if you're on your way to a world already sunk
in the hot night of empty hands.
Or if you advance toward the walls of time
like a dream in which you believe you're exhaling
the savage nature of secret things.
Here I will be able to listen to your crying,
your bright and womanly flame, your pride
of a bird plunging into rotten water.
Come, Robinson, approach the garden of other delights.
Now your planet, that small territory where
your name collected the weight of the chosen, is strange.
Be dazzled by the seagull's cry.
You will no longer perish, there will no longer be moon and
    sun,
roots to preserve the thirst of those who live alone.

III

Goddess of an arrested time in the window.
Bitter forecasts. Winters eroded
in the salt from a door of light and glass.
I am not mistaken.
I know sand's dreamscapes are sad,
the tracks we leave little by little,
like a landscape tattooed on the skin of insomniacs.

The chairs of time that once supported the figure
of a farmer sowing in rain are broken.
Once again it was Virgil and his severed pledge,
whitecaps as old as the forest floor,
boars and lionesses yoked together and an immense
half-pruned elm that stayed like this with the power
of the dead Latin in your notebooks.
Conquered are the rocking chairs
where we rock a dead child back and forth
to the coo of mother vipers,
mother snakes, mothers without mothers,
orphans of delirium, and in that tepid bunk
we could hide tributes of dust and ash.
Domestic Robinson, computer of lives
and soliloquies, grinder of promises
in pages upon pages of your literature.
I've watched you meditate, prince of night.
I've been able to listen to your bones' misplacement,
particles of line to feed the raven,
ligaments of torpor and vigilance resisting
the lunatic's brutal wallop and squawk: never more.
I can see your darkened blood, your mouth blue
from time and that deaf heart where shadow
was the filament of a thousand years of galleries and
      enclosures.
I have been able to watch your country of foam and the
      foliage
that covers your most beloved dreams
as if you still lived in that privileged place.

IV

Come along, come with me to hear the laughter of sorrows.
let us look at the children's celestial map.
One must engineer phrases for your island, amnesiac stones
installed with the harness of the faded ones.
Don't allow the sea to diminish in its own unspoken secret.
No, Robinson. History is something else.
It is a hole in the mouth of nobody.
The nothingness we all know is part of our nonsense.
Evening will always be poised on the tip of the tongue,
a sunlit insult where pelicans and seagulls
dispute the thirst of whoever refuses to admit
the ant's victory over the soil.
Dawn's sweet proposals.
The world, the entire world is a black sphere,
a dreadful strain to destroy a shadow,
that old she-wolf guarding our wound.
I am not mistaken when I say that the word grace
incites laughter in lonesome men.
I have heard them and among them
You have crossed out amazement's finest salt
with a simple song, an absurd cooing
or an absurd plan to be an adventurer.
But for what? From which of this life's shores?
Nobody has granted you permission and you
have taken those black suns
as if they were part of your life,
the foolishness of a thought
that will never be extinguished.

V

Listen, listen to time's detonations.
Don't confuse the aviator's signs
with booming that begins on the tongue.
Powerful provocations. Time of scales.
Skin's filth and stubble.
And at the beach?
People constantly dock in other abysses.
They emerge. They split up. They do what they may.
Allow for a dispelled spirit's murmurs
to return to you as shells to sand.
There will be neither frogs nor luminaries like fierce Ulysses.

Tap-tap-tap
goes the sound of the sky's falling tears.
Panic's labyrinth lost
between your tongue's alphabets.
Tap that disagreement with the animals
crossing the border.
Tap: days to come and those gone by,
terminal waters of a youngster
astonished in the sun's first light.
Tap: sounds of dresses falling at the drinking fountains
of the fugitive and friends.
Tap: tiny particles that crack
in a metal and emerald sky.
Tap: that castle of truth and thought
built from the saliva of sluggish mates.

Tap: the catafalques and apiaries where crazies cry
alongside widows stalemated by war.

Leave now, Robinson, leave your lair.
Sail different oceans where you may ply
through the serenity of a clear forecast.

VI

All of them are already gone. Your companion
with blue ibis feathers and your dog.
The erotic seashell open to your island's purity,
your carriage of dreams and its cotton landscapes,
the trains that shine even in that dark.

Now leave your silence and that tree growing immense
in its transparency. No consequence
will be the measure of a new world,
your whales' ecstatic castle.
There is no greater poem than the blue graveyard of beauty.
If you return here you'll see the shape of another century.
the brief interval that dilates the hours of our bones.
Remember that the size of death is never the same.
Its space is always in the awful stammering
that we are all bound to hear.
You will long for a time when a palm and its creaking
were a bonfire, that true pulse
that announced your home to you. And the always
trembling air would surprise you with its salty, tropical

breath, its burning love in earthy passion.
Distant dawns. Parts of the sun in your throat.
Birds from other heavens that you considered
siblings and friends, lavish glow of a log
and insect emancipations. Tree bark.
Amputations of lime among seaside plants.
Spells. And that crazy star that prefigured
the bouts between your head and heart.
Such delirium.

Someone broke the rope of your planet's light.
It will not be vision that goes with you
like drumbeats publicizing dawn.
That is vertigo: to stand alone and survey
a paradise at the edge of memory.

VII

Who remains? Who do you leave behind your yellowed atlas
when you go? Your parasol and hat. Vine on the hill
like a victory of your new century. Small goat
like a whisper that corresponds to your desire.
You await your incredible city full of echoing voices.
Its constituents don't register in your memory, they don't
        quake
for you, they don't protect you. Slow now are the angry pages
where alone they scrub their pornography.
You'll find no trace of them in a raindrop. No trace.
Now all of us people, holes without memory,

would live below ground looking in the subsoil for a word,
Perhaps a fragment of fortune to allow us to speak
openly about a secret syllable.
This war and the sea's overwhelming saltpeter are strange.
And not ours. Insects nourished by someone else's substance.
They imitate a dry leaf's rare perfection. They consume.
There are larvae and nymphs. They bore a hole in the tree
for their young. Shims. Extensions. Parts of a faith
with rotten roots. They expand. They consume a portion
of an apocryphal paradise. And are sustained. They eat with
    pleasure.
They are nourished by meat and fresh fruit. Then the sea
comes to rest far from dreams. And echoes.
Open the door: use your hands to untie
the fields and flower gardens, the blue forests of tamarinds.
The bee will come and steal your knife.
The tapirs will come to lick your wound.
The eagles will come to remove your light
and you will lose your regal head, ruler of your own blunder.

VIII

Don't let anyone tell you what to do. Stand guard at the exits
of your indulgence. White termite mounds for your desire's
    salt.
Ample obstacles. Sacraments.
Thorny chains of suffering gather in your visions'
endless embrace. Have no fear. There will always be a good
    day

to speak with the wave and with the foam, with the fish that
   design
battles in which a reptile hides in the mud.
Stupidity and madness for whoever uses someone else's
keyboard to compose music. Renditions of laughing cats
calling upon tile roofs. Wailing.
No tiger exists to secure your suspicion. There is no fire.
Demand the thirst that cuts stones and hieroglyphs at dawn.
Saturn in your notebook.
Now there is no gold to saturate your heart. There's nothing.
The blue is intense. You can't distinguish
The void's southern region.
Pale salt auctions
on a castaway's skin. Save the land.
I listen to dawn's arrangements
in the soft beating of its moans.
And you go on still alone. You no longer dream.
It's enough for you to create secret webs
from earth's ephemeral buds. You adjust.
You allow fever to cover your roots. And you keep on.
Within your speech the ocean gently stirs.
The century passes beyond you. It is the sign,
the first sign of your ghosts. Who follows you?
Narrator of big promises I have seen you rouse dawn
from beneath the mollusk's useless creaking. Which moment
of desperation was yours? How many earthly complaints
did you gather among praise's flexible folds?

IX

Thirst grinds against public opinion.
Your anonymous and submissive public.
Omens of a faith that gets the better of bullies.
You open the hypocrite's skin one flake at a time
on a bed of algae. Old literary passages
leak like juice from a polyp.
A face improvises with its thousand radiant disguises.
The old man who offers you a foot massage walks by,
in your tracks and your shoes of lime and song
that always perforate the future's mirror
with a face. Depositions. Crusts.
Coatings of salt and signs. Green declarations
of the world and its renunciations. Horoscopes.
Kites of smoke. Foam lifting in the air
of restless fish, fish of light
that wait in your dreams.
Your home left behind in a battle.
Half of paradise forgotten
like an extinguished torch.
You melt gold on a snowy road. And you use it up.
You guard a mountain's treasure. You're a catalyst
gathering and congregating the laypeople of the land.
Red ants in pilgrimage to your cave.
You itch as your saliva's joy
inflames your story's beginnings.
You're the precise owner, joy's perfect geometrician,
campesino anxious to see his rock,

eagle's shriek at the sacrifice of its daughters.

You have seen twelve revolving doors collapse. The moss that
might

have revived your hills is gone. Now the earth hides its crazy,

greedy tasks, braiding laurel into the stillness of morning.

You decide to arrange your goat's intestines around your
neck.

You simulate a night of openhearted love.

Birds sing to you.

Your memory is the country of sinister shadows.

From Avid World

Translated by Aurelia Cortés Peyron
and María Richardson

> *A rumor travels over land and seas.*
> —Propertius

Mother, in summer at times
the world is a wasp,
nomad, iridescent. We talk
birds,
crisp birds,
they fly inside shade and us. Is it
possible?
Veins were in
the wax of July
and the pots
of flowers and dew,
the warm perfumes of drones
and virgins. Ocarinas, always.

Mother, cover the sour mist
and the deluge, rub,
rub one day
on another.
There are larvae in the earth,
margins—that I will never leave,
pergolas, broken
glass, silken slander
on the walls. Shards
and subterranean edges. Muscles.
Oils: there are spears,
holes (an immense

and deliberate cave,
a hollow.) They knock, they wait.

No. No, it's nobody.
Say: Is it
a coincidence?

There are lindens in my text, clover and filaments.
Fermentations. Old fermentations
(they knead them, pile them, mother, tear them apart)
and the distance that
blooms perfectly
unique and my sisters?

I know.
Fragile, ephemeral, tiny and almost
possible there was
a flower
in permanence:
past and future for us.
I kept cabbages. Mother,
did I fail?

I

And we learned the future on limestone over rock
the rust of knowing that we were
an open gap for insects to cross,
the only light on the tip of our tongues,

the ever delayed moaning in the silence,
a body, and another, and another where the night
officiated songs of peace over dead leaves.
And slow we walked on the bright red
of a flower that opened its lavish petals
only during Lent. And we saw wild boars
drinking the quiet word sun,
bee lanterns, dead rivers
on loosened weeds, caravans
of ants like a spot of restlessness,
a stroke of shivering
where light felt like a sentence fragment.
And on the edge of a wind-conceived
breathing sky we saw
the hastened flight of our shadows,
those lots of bread and mud where we said
world for the first time.

II

World as truth,
as barren fog
microscopic in the stillness of dust.
And a strong smell of fat woke us up
in a place imagined by dawn.
Echoes torn in rings of smoke.
Words carved in stone
confident like a snake dreaming
nobody's dream. Questions,

plasters on old scars
take form in the eye's perception.
Traces of a foreign hope,
continuously postponed footprints
at the beginning of the journey.
The shadow unfolds
next to the cry of a bird of prey.
Who is who in this jungle?

III

Saddles on skin. Saturations.
Hundreds of butterflies
look after the blue sleep of their chrysalis.
Deserters of other clouds
they keep paper planes
in their gold retinae.
Prevarications of a time
when rain was the gestation
of an undefined plant.
We waited until dawn
for the eagle's cry
if only to know
it was time to listen
to the fragments of a story
with broken hope.

IV

That they should take us
over the seas of grass.
That they should bring us up
in the wings of dream, to the place of coated
pupils.
That they should clear all of a sudden
the clamor of the air and the eye
of their offering.
May angels and monsters bloom
in the white night
of the scale.
May undeniable childhood
become a river of voices, a choir
of laughter in pollen grains.
May the hunger of grasslands
be benevolent to the dream
of the snake.
May rituals of peace and song
gather on the warrior's lip.
From this lip,
as if it was a sea from afar
may the writing of the poem spring.

VI

And the moon with its borrowed fire
cries until we're undone:

Misery! Misery!
I raised my eyes and saw the loneliness
of an almost branch, a little branch
revealed, a branch lost in immensity,
a possible encounter with that
ardent servant, chronicler
of a made-up death.
But blindly, under the untamed
moonlight,
I could see the branch, the little branch
revealed, a branch lost in immensity
hanging imperishable from within, smothered
by the weeping air, in the pit of uncountable
time, pretending,
pretending it was a crowd
in the mood of darkness.
The branch then wanted to creak,
horrid like entrails or an unfaithful
pulse of dream and I saw
for an instant the sadness
of a life of fleeing,
fleeing from the fall
alone
like an almost branch of misery.

IX

How can I write about you
without it being unbearable?

How can I say your name,
Lacandonia,
between my open eyelids?
How can I speak your laughter, your
hangman body in the thickets?
How to praise your lioness noises,
your shadow roar
that startles barn owls?
How to dream your long days
immersed in me,
in my drowsiness of ruins?
How to scream your cloud
at the mirror that looks at me
like a ghost
of another era?
How to drink your open syllables?
How to lick your wafers
of kindness and belonging?
How to implore you, unmoving,
the thirst of being
the voice of a robin,
the scorching fire that burns
in the lines of your music?

X

Ravel on your mind. One sound purer than the next
on the shirt that covers the epiphyte plants.
Light inverts on the minister's hands,

the blue officiant admiring nature
and securing its nourishment. All he receives
is the use of a secret life: nectar, honey,
delicacies of resin and bark. And in the intact
joints of his name, tambourines and rattles
and perhaps a long chord to greet the wind.
You take notes: for you, a bird is a string,
the anonymous bed of any fortitude.
Vertebrae, arms, and nooks of the body
accomplish the mute
movement of the voice in your head.
And this eagerness, almost bound to simulation
makes you put to bed the dreams
of cubs and offspring, of the many birds
that own you
in the immensity of your jungle.

XII

(*For Emilio*)

The music that officiates
is an absence,
an unseen vision,
the light that plunges
a bird of smoke.
Torrential music
carves its countenance,
its figure,

its plains of stars,
its not saying a river
if for him it has
the voices of another
conceited river
fathered by his fingers,
as if it was song and lyrics
of naiads imploring God,
the flight of storks,
maybe a perfect and errant sound like dew
over the eternal feather
of its body.

XIV

From the depths. From illicit bodies
that fall and open. From their fruit.
From fire to fire, and from one lightning
to another to another. From what lies between
you and the lightness of dark.
From deep valleys. From what hurts
the eye and causes a stream of smell.
From your bitterness and your ether mouth.
From what pushes and shakes, and is distant, there,
in front, like the future. From what fulfills
and slips into the juice.
From what moves away and smashes into your treetops
of air. From what is flat and remote, continuous
and dry in the loamy mask of a sturdy

mare. From what collects pollen and brags,
and labializes every which way
on its path. From what lacerates
and directs hidden in its hole. From what
pours and shines like a black way
through open shadows. From the explosion
of silencing the name of its fruit,
of its illicit bodies, of the depths.

XVII

Open, Stone, your night.
Leave my mouth, forgive
the song of glass, the gluttony
of seeing, the zest of being
silent. Silence, Stone,
my eyes inside you, file
your arrogant skin,
let me admire
your female bird line,
and blow away fearful
your writing of air,
your tidy thirst
of being paradise.
Pull out from me,
in my entrails
this grafted sun
tongue, a tongue of burning
grass. That no one see

your mute face, Stone
on earth, break
the stanza of the day
that slowly fades
and rule, Stone, entirely,
the bed of the world,
string of light for the blind.

From Dylan and the Whales

Translated by Forrest Gander

> *a hole of errands and shades*
> —Dylan Thomas

> *What sounds are those, Helvellyn, that are heard?*
> —William Wordsworth

I

What are they, Dylan, those sounds come down to us
from the white forest
of your watery mouth?

What burning lime did you kindle
back in your city made from time
gone blank?

What stone disgorged for you
the howl of that Herod of straw and salt
who whisked up your blood?

What stumbling saint
already undone among the warm veins
that perforate your wound?

Seaward,
by owl-light
it's my life imagined
by the force of a dead man,
a precarious prince on the sky's shore,
who gives me leave to address myself to the soldier's fire,

enables me to pronounce my shadow over the water's
    debauchery
where to name the light is to draw the night,
to open the calyx to dawn's reason.

Here death maintains its dominion,
where someone, maybe a slave
god of rain,
a forgotten monarch of such things,
eagerly opens himself to blood's silence
in the vertigo and fear of the night
to say that he goes, that he burns deep
in cups of dust in which his thirst drips away inside a vacuum.

This is the hour in which I know
the broken part of my story,
a fragment chiseled on suicide's chill night.

My body contains a sick prayer,
a story dug from a clout of earth.
My body keeps a lost prayer
under shade beggared by dogs and children.
My life holds a thistle feast
in the dream of its skull
and a blind image that lies down
deep and invincible
in the sterile memory of days.
For eyes, I have two gardens and for a mouth,
a sun announcing the fire in the tide.

The field of my childhood is now
a round place where my heart
palpitates with the blood of the hills.
I have no other light than the river
that slinks into the sky of all my years
under this sun
that, caught on time's crest, might reappear.
I cling to no other reason than to sing to him,
to the last Odysseus of the fields, happy child
and wild as a blind horse in the meadow.
I live on thunder's lip,
where to eat a piece of bread
is to deprive the ants of their conjugal air,
where to say I have nothing
is like licking the cup of tempestuous valleys,
fear's unforgettable swamp.

I have here what was once a death apart from me,
a profound life with no one to give me air,
sky, sun or the impetus to remain in just one form,
open unparalleled clarity, where what resounds
is my poor wandering fish of a heart among men
that it might praise the appearance of rain
and earth's newly birthed face.

Here they scream *love* to say poor and they iterate
the echoes of stones and dust until finally they uproot
the sky from the day's birds.
Here to live is to do so apart from the men

whittled into these peaceable rocks
of lies and of flesh.
Here they say *voice* and the wind just takes off,
they say *peace* and from a fountain bubbles that scarlet dew
that leaks darkness over the luckless born to this arid ground
inhabited by worms and eccentrics
who chatter at the stones
and guard, between the tombs,
the tender quietude of their secrets,
the particular tune of their blood.
It's a colorless land already worn out and yet
there's a tepid frog croaking, between sips of soda,
in the breath of men sweating out their memories,
between knots in clothes hung up by young girls
and among children lost in the dust
of grocery bags.
It's a land without pity where men sing
to reasonable dawns and chickens peck the clouds,
accomplices to the bustling afternoon.
Here the skin of a tree is blessed
and it's the rain — an awakening for the ducks —
and it's the air, that shriek of truth
aimed toward the red kites,
in the feast of being a man among men
who trail after their lives
on some tidy hill or in a dark cavern,
where maybe she can always be found,
where she speaks.

III

You listen for voices: salt sheets for your voice on fire.
You hear the wind break into you with its green wings
rotting in the mud.
You understand it's the plan of fragile and
simple gods.
Your restlessness calls to your mind
the interior of a forest screaming through its insects.
Dissonant and harmonic creatures announcing to you
the first unreachable moment when children are born.
Authentic time derived from an anonymous rib
in steady stabs, some sweet imitation of eagerness
for the monasticism of the dying.
The wind goes to pieces in your head.
It brings to mind a song on the crucifixion
that comes and goes in your sex.
You say Christ struggled with his loves
and the famous thorn
nailed to his chest's song.
The robin comes nearer. The land empties out
and you prophesy blood running through the streets
in order to be, by your own mouth, who you are,
equanimous and beaten,
balancing yourself on the stone of temptations.
Like him, you glorify yourself.
You hang a blue sign at the entrance to your cave.

There's no crow that endures through its squawks
the invocation of dust and ash.

The face of a witch is prophesied.
There are Celtic legends oozing
through the skin of your son: Beowulf buried
with the dragon's treasure at his chest,
the nobles of the rose with their long hair
racing through the field,
Saint Telmo lost in a grain of sand.
There are vagrant trails left by fantastic ships,
the route to Santiago is one vast rumor
where the soul is laid waste,
and "Shut up, my sweet!"—
you urge the whining vagrant wandering
by the fairies' green caves
and the illicit rivers where night strips down.
You sing.
You sing through the eyelids of a word in your spit.
An armor mask guards your name,
your soldier's name,
your father's name given to gaze at the whales
as if they were undulating candles.
You cry beneath the moon's grimaces
on the eve of alum.
Two by two you arrive at March
from March to the vulva of every rigging.
The rats and the chancres are the opacity on the bay.

And in that darkness
where the saints ring their bells
you look to sate your thirst with a gulp of seawater
that collects in the flower of your throat.

You drink, you drink a bit of life
dancing among the shadows of all your ghosts.

IV

And if what you see on your face were the sea?
The murderous sea with its voice of dust and poverty.
The sea that killed Manuel and lost Juan's body.
The sovereign sea that goes down before the poem.
That to which you cannot return.
The sea you sip with your child's voice,
scion of the night, ram at noon,
I don't want to see your black breath shushing the guts
piled into the baptismal font,
I don't want to wake and see you there on the ranch
like some open chalice between wormy fruits.

Let them rise from your thirst, the harvests of pride
and the time of a lapidary god
with a falcon eye and a lightning finger
pointing out that weedy dam
from where the cranes of faith sing to you.

Let the nervous root rise
with the trace of the siren,
the sludge of the unicorn,
the innocence of the nettle,
let the ice and hail spill
over the withered trees of the whimper.

Let raving packs of dogs completely
vanish into the silence

and humidity of their summers,
may they back off from the tuneless mother,
the poorly loved wife,
the zodiac's fists
and the peasant who is your father.

Let the vipers' tongues squirm away,
the gunpowder of the bitter girl,
the mother
and the thief of your verses and your tears,
let them all go.

Let go the ones who confuse their own face
with the furrows in the field
and the feast of the jubilant thistle,
and the mother,
let her go.

Let the first son go,
and the second son, and the third,
with their mother's smacks to your temples,
let them go.

Let them leave you with the white and yellow sea,
with its sand cove and its salt bank,
with its austere throng and its voice—hoarse
and red and sleepy—and its time line.
Its string and its shells,

its long reefs for peace and silence
and its time-torch and its time-altar
and its time-sandal
and its fetid stink of time.

Let them leave you alone and blessed
by the murmur of the golden, gentle sea
and its quilted spectra and its eyelids
and its death date stamped on its secret son.
Let them leave you.

V

A twenty-four-hour-old angel has come your way
to lick your veins,
to scorch clouds
and lightning in the dampness of your sleep,
to test your dark hero's blood
with a cyclone of wings
over gravestones that fume in your sleep,
in your child-sleep,
the sleep of a bird lost on the first night of dreams.

A twenty-four-year-old angel has come your way
and squawks like some night-animal in the *detritus*
where the silent fish inflaming
your journey bleed out.
The fish of your life
have come to be that angel stranded on your tongue
when the girls went lost in some wasteland
behind the dry hill
while you,
ardent and legendary,
hunted for traces of coal beneath that angel's good luck.

How many times did you leap up at midnight
in response to a cry,
even a wail of madness,
from milky grass where the rivers cross.

Now you only have a shattered sky,
a lying tongue bleeding between the thistles
and a pigsty where you cuddle
the sterile voice of a girlfriend who brags,
among the pigs, that she's your one and only.

How many times did the shriek of the parrot and the child
leave you starved and seated at a table
loaded with death's meadows
at the fork of a venomous hive.

How many times did you cut living branches
whipping-up lightning and sparks,
what plenitude danced for you
on the bones of a broken doll.

What pleasure severe as the rooster's song
and the eye of the gypsy
who reads in your palm the word *end*
in a ravine of constellations.

What hand more powerful than that of the guardian angel
who swats down once and again your crumbling city.

Your stone angel in the belfry of time.
Your angel of exultation who awaits you
like a voracious octopus in the open seas.

Your angel of a woman's glove
since no one dirties your quiet grave
where the bones of your anonymous voice go dry before love
    does.

It has come to you in an assassin's shroud,
the canvas where the eye and the folds and the mouth
are the false bonds of those who ask for love
by asking for death.
It has come.
It has come to you and it drives you mad.

Sanctum sanctorum.

VII

For about a minute you spin
and the world shifts galaxies.
What germinates in your flesh is the viper's dream.
You slither through the underbrush
praying for the abolition of mornings,
in a wisp of water you abandon yourself.
You think life is easy
if men withdraw from History:
you'd like to forget the crowd,
the exile's glass which desecrates your face
and your shriveled illusion.
Nothing you have is part of your life.
Something was stolen from you in childhood.
That's why the rain holds off and the sea,
when you notice it,
bellows at you.
Every animal lasts for a while
on your tongue.
Over the invisible shacks birds call to you
come on, it's time to get down to the killing,
you add your song to the psalms of widows
and you offer a sacrifice
at the weddings of autumn and earth.

Huge tufts of durable peace fall
like installments on the sadness of leaves.
White is the rain at dawn

and white the mothers who wake to it.
A rejection of momentum waits to ambush the child's heart.

You vie with yourself over whether virtue exists.
You remain at the edge of the age
where there's an unimproved room.
You can't understand the silence.
Your mode of fidelity is to stretch out a sheet
between death and the water.

Outside, the whales seem like tears
trekking life's terse skull.

VIII

I've safekept your foamy mask between my teeth.

I've eaten from your cold ladle of marrow
and tasted your old sepulchral blood
in a garden that even now is vanishing.

I've waited for late ships to be ambushed at twilight
in order to lick at the thirst of the vanquished, the plank
   of bitterness
from which you, in your cripple's shoes, stepped out.

Impatiently I left you that soft skin
ripped from your brief childhood,
I took your crib as if it were my lair
and I flew off fast—away from my destiny,
the unfettered madwoman who gave birth to scorpions
while listening to the song and the trembling of those little
   faithless
and childless widows. For you, the hand shoved
through the sea's lapel shines through cracks
in a fecund constellation beyond the eyes of the blind.
For your sake the light, tired of expanding
the earth's white dunes,
disseminates misfortune's scent so one day
below the rocks, those who were shipwrecked might emerge
   from you
and come to be your voice, singular and sane,

because next comes the age when the deserving come back
here among life's green bulbs.

Because whatever was before doesn't keep on,
through the night of vivid screams,
as a basin for some god to trace out his breath
in the shape of a scythe and so guide us
to you, to me and my enemy,
under the eyelids of a sick sun,
obscurity and storm
between the lips of a childhood
in which faces were the rope
connecting man and beast,
so we might know we were the compass
of a timeless time between two bodies.

Pull, only pull is what you call out, but there's a fish
in the cold splash of living water which reminds you
of what you are to him at the feast of an assassin bird.

I can't see what you see because in my fear
there's a lamp that swallows, in the ritual of being,
a dry-mouthed penitent,
a clay body standing erect,
that it might name the dark peace of thunder,
the abyss's soul,
and so to be able to overcome that quick instant of swamp
that makes us feel that you, me, all the others
are a single unique moment, unlit, hesitant.

Because I knew that my life
was for safekeeping victory's fine salt
and for walking then across the acid ground of silence
where my heart fumed in the light
body after body like a wet-nurse
who breastfeeds her pack of vipers.

And I knew then how to see in whatever remains distinct
     and apart
the fresh immolation of constancy,
just as the sea and its stubble meet
the day's age each afternoon,
and so I established in that fire
my home and my ration of life.

Look at me now here as I restore
in the horror and helplessness
of nobodies for whom to be someone
for whatever or whenever
means to enter into the kingdom of birds, to dream
that we have neither pigs nor men who tire of shouting
their secrets up at some stained glass of a god
no one recognizes.

My loyal heart,
fugitive and open to undulant sounds,
searching out a place of warm contrasts
where it can scream

between thick crusts of its own blood.
My heart, a small chalice open to the precipice,
in latrines full of love and celestial blue.
In its want of love my sullen heart
shudders, its ambition overturned
so violently
it drops a little, vertiginous,
into the bitter salt that stings the vanquished.

XI

Who crowns lonely kings?
Who bleeds them?
Mud-animals pierce the perfume
in the poet's word,
a fire in the incest of its lost constellation.
The mythical animals surround your tomb, Dylan Thomas,
shepherd of felines,
god of the crazy and of the cyanide mouth.
Voice, the only voice of things.
You christen the water at the coronation of a sacrifice.
You drink the tempest in the auguries
and your word buds like spring in the wasteland.
From the word, an eternity of substance,
time scarring the blanched recollection
of those who have drowned,
the fruit's overly bitter emission
beneath the vomitous eye.
From the word, the erect sign of the fleshy and lobed plant
where man appears as a firebird
crossing the pale sky.
From the word the contours of the heart of the destitute,
the impetus of the servant of a faltering god,
the cove and clod of the filthy magnicide.
From the word the light of those missing
from kitchens where the grace of absence
boils, the easy happiness
under night's scalded pore

and a mare's
infection there in the stable of the missing.
For November's sake
before a rump risen in dampness,
when the old man acquiesces to caresses,
to the white flowers protected
by mercy's sweet oration.
From the word the shovel of that old man who digs
down to find the green fruit
of plainest incredulity.
From the word, the hitman's misery,
his trusty habit of burying his pay between the intact
leaves of his Bible and the tremor crossing a fake earth.

Your word is already part of the tribe.
And I do not know why the night
arrived so suddenly to blot out everything.
Who murdered my history?
Who tells lies for the lost?

XII

I don't know your country, Dylan Thomas, and yet
I've seen your mountains bloom in the sun at morning
the farmed lands that rise out
of an ancient dawn to bless
the children's naked skin,
the cliffs where blind widows weep
and let their wailing escape
into the voice of the thunder,
the pendent clouds that extend their dominion
in lines staged by the starving,
the caverns where men hoard
their indelible treasures,
their shares of misery and paradise
where wolves lick at the fever of the banished.
I've seen the high piles of meat carved
for whomever makes out the marks of those dying,
abominably, in the thirst of a bed.
I have seen the crazy kid and the sick woman
lurching through the streets of your town
searching for an angelic place, a feather,
where they might fall before a god
whose cloak is kissed, on a bale of rocks.
I have seen your world age,
its star teetering off course,
and the word "Order" and the word "Faith"
which slandered you so badly in your dreams,
now they are guileless serpents

shielded behind the pulpit
of an alien man.
I've seen the shadow of your friends
with their raven wings spurring on the prodigals:
their two feet amputated, their hands dried up
in the delirium of an imprisoned wind.
I've seen your country
turn into tears for the disappeared,
seen the children of your children
taking succor forever on their knees in the dirt.
I've seen the lugubrious closing of your fiery eyelids
so that they don't shame your daughters.
Seen fools and giants, the barely there and the awful,
the mournful and exalted falling furious,
mouth to mouth against the floor,
in the thickness of its broken lie,
gnawing at the skin of a single bone.
Maybe that's why you stand apart, Dylan Thomas,
perhaps maybe you won't pass this way again
where the crowds make a lone hill,
where a blazing heart
is ensconced in the word "Secret."
Perhaps you think it's all a life of fiction
and the world plots its conspiracy.

Maybe you're right and we,
the solitary ones, our bones
loaded with an oblivious hope,
we've been benighted bit by bit.

XV

Near here is your house.
Very close to the moss and dry grass,
where swallows scrawl their futures across the air,
where the luxury of the oppressed
is drinking a glass of wind
and the sovereigns are sure
of living in peace.

Near here is your house.
It's a little hole in the sand of no one
and yet, from there, you see the waves
of your childhood sea,
the burning assassin's desert night.
There you can listen to a Godless race
wailing to the infinite,
falling into an emptiness sucked up
into the ranks of buffoonery.
Your eyes hear time's erosion,
the multiple meanings of cat's claws,
the biblical quotation, the man's confession
and the divine choir of the illustrious
singing to the open space that begs freedom for the just,
clemency for the tormented,
a voice for the centaur's dewy liberator.
Because man's blind ownership
makes him distrustful in the Hollands of night,
afraid between pauses in the flesh,

he comes to forget the brutality
of being a kid under the tree of the poor.

For whom do we pretend to bow to the abyss,
that we can gaze at the faces of the goldsmith when he cries,
that we hear the song of the mutilated in its silence,
that we know the pain of a mother
abandoned to her son's sterility.
For whom do we pretend if we're still no one
but want to see the covenantal root
in the sweet roar of words.
Who can we ask to uncover the bones of their children,
to pack up the ashes
that sustain the lie or the truth
of innocuous kings and detestable elders.

To whom can it be said that life is one single moment
in the time of our kind.

XVI

Never have I touched the sea or its insubstantial skin
       which embroiders the sacred.
Never have I touched the dreamy sand of the beach
where birds keep guard over their own thinness.
Not once have I listened to the stealthy
crowd of waves.
nor to the painful wallop coming from behind the mountain.
But I've dreamed, ah, Dylan Thomas, I've dreamed
of the salt of apparitions
and time's fruitful fall into my hands.
I've swallowed ocean water all alone screaming
through my eyes and my split ends and my wrinkled body
and my vanquished hair which ignites
the foam in my throat.
Because I've been the antihero
who travels through silence kept by that sea, the word.
The one evincing the scent of algae
on the table of sacrifices.
Here too we nourish the idiom of the clown and the afflicted.
Here the picklock for the skin of Virgilians,
the nettle's piercing silence.
Here the wind's *detritus* and the countenance of some tracks
circling back into a fable.
Here wild green is the color of prophets
who devise frayed Aeneids
charged with the rage of those who adored travelers.
Here is everything in its distinctness . . .

We've lost so many phoenixes that the eagle's cry
becomes a daily prayer and the blackbird
with its cackling dark voice
kneels in the night
on the blanket of the damned.

You've come this far Dylan Thomas just to see the dream
that dreams you howling into tomorrow:
it's a dream of a tiger in the summer of your blood.
A tiger with candle eyes and a water face.
A rain-in-your-throat tiger that loathes the valleys
of the imagination, the agonizing badlands
of burning memory.
A tiger of lime and obsidian, its stripes in the shadow
of a tomb. The tomb that awaits you,
the hard white tomb with its white certainty and its worms
in the briefness of that vertigo now gnawing at your fables.
Your horrific fables so like the tears of archangels
that irrigate rivers and forests, their edges invaded
by red puddles of hollow words.
Words that sting men, that singe the loneliness
there in the saltpeter, that spike the insurgent saliva
of those who don't even know
the language of the rose and the orchid.

Stainless steel words
in which the peasant's thirst flickers out
and the children's hunger goes mute beneath their tears.

XVII

You hear a Bengal tiger.
It's come down with the gannets
to lick that chord of flying fish.
You imagine a heart within the beating foam.
What ripples over the water, that's the thirst of your visions:
the ceremony of cut bamboo
for cleaning up the blackened blood
there in the sacks,
the island protected by a little insect
with its black striations fading out,
a leech that still can be heard
on these nights marked by rain and white nightmares
in the drunken procession of what we love
and in that awful memory that pries open your eyes
and scalds your tongue in the harpoon ritual.
How sweet to pronounce your name
in the peace accompanying a steamboat,
such huge pathos in a verbal climate that undoes you,
and so to be able to lick the beggar's cross and the false word,
the latter tossed out with ratflesh.

All night it rains with a solidity
that only girls cherish.
All the fecund night, the smoke of your dreams and your sex:
you can't forget the assertion made by the one you're ripping
     to shreds.
A tiger congeals between your lips

as the night's blood runs out
through your eyelids.
An accident-prone tiger goes to pieces
when dawn's train roars through
only to hiss out in the water.
A Bengal tiger falls through a sewer
and its howl disperses
in the fog and inflames a scavenger's heart.
A tiger for you is just a river of light,
a line no one will cross ever again to feed you.
A tiger for you is only a cat,
a century of victory for the old claws of your eyes.

What gets dropped is always a part of your speech.
In the winter a farmer takes pleasure in your delirium.
What leaves gets lost between your warm moans.
Maybe the moon doesn't press on after that Bengal tiger
but allows you to be the pure rumor any soul can discover.
Here blood tastes like secret salt.
You tear open a feral cat and you eat it without groaning
    without losing heart.
"I beg God for help," you shout to us,
"just to quench my thirst in the rigging."
Thirst is there in the flaming tribute
spreading across the meadow of lime in a tub with no mosaics.
Thirst's body is a slot in the skin behind the neck
and its stretch marks make you think once again of that solitary
    tiger
going down to the river to lick up the blood of the one you love.

XX

Shh Shhh Shhhh

I command you to shut up. It's Prince
Beowulf unleashed on the heart of dawn.
And everything starts up again
and again and again
"as once it was."
You cross the sea to the land of the Danes.
You tear open the wound.
Life becomes a dot at the horizon,
a cry the truth allows,
in his fierceness, he lines up
and scouts for the outbreak,
the signal where emptiness
offers him a place to bleed out his form.
He's lost his throne.
His throne of seeds and his inmate's pallet,
his throne enchanted by apology's god,
the god of cement
along a curved shore,
a god of worm-eaten wood shouting at us:
All clarity comes from vertigo.

And it was like a final farewell voyage:
the ship with its banner in a gold mount,
his sword, his helmet and his shield,
horns for drinking up the time

and the seed of the years.
It took place in the River Deben estuary in Suffolk,
where the animals
plod through mud
and Christians bury their crazies.
So the nightmare repeats itself:
the women weeping to their children.
Now they're weeping in Kosovo.
The empty faces, the clocks, the bell towers, the birds
agitated, avid to find a chink in the waters.
All clarity comes from vertigo.
Again and again it begins
"as once it was":

the misery sustained by an old man
who has lived to see the body of his son
swing at the gallows. And who starts to cry, to recite
a funereal song for his child, gaping at the crow
savagely exultant in the dangling shadow.

Blissful Beowulf
who strolls down the street to heal himself of nothing.
Because he owns nothing and is frank and beautiful and
    mysterious.
His body in my body frustrates oblivion.
"I have two owls for daughters." He sings to me.
He tells me about some trace of tincture and vinegar
subsumed into the flesh of the vanquished.
He says there's a garden where flowers are hearts

on fire for nobody's eyes. So he says. He says that.
And mentions thorns. And enchantments that net
the dreams of birds,
ruins laid open to legends of wind,
arrogant and whispery branches lurking in the nose
of a lunatic who goes around without a tie.
He mentions storms,
still water in the exhausted atmosphere.
Everything that withdraws is lost as far off
as thirst at the horizon,
as the clouds drawn up slowly
into a girl's braids.
He mentions fatigue,
he acknowledges the quiet rumor of returns,
the story of a throne misplaced in a ravine,
the silent temple of predators,
time's pigsty in which some god
fornicated mutely,
the prayer of suicides.
He speaks of abysses,
awestruck times in urinals and at banquets
where the sun plows its errant ulcers into tin cans
and cigarette butts.
He says that when the sun sinks it dives deep into night's river.
He knows he won't look back.
He'll shout that life is a last breath.
And that all clarity comes from vertigo.
All.

XXI

Today I've spent the morning beside you Dylan Thomas.

There was a washed-out oval image, eternally white.
It was an eye open
to useless things blown away by the wind,
to days slowly trudging to the slaughter,
to the shout of dawn shaving itself on the sidewalks,
to the money that heals poverty,
to the mutilation and neglect that keeps a wife
dressed in some greasy cloth,
to the final day when a boy leaves home and won't return
to the chief's cry, to the gentle scratching of some crazed bitch.

Yes, that eye open to the century ending
already weary of the uselessness and of the empty sound of
    deaf words.
That century stinking of shit and hospital, with a dead rat in
    the trauma wing.

It stinks like a wall gone quiet in the air's detonation,
in the perfect form of silence. It stinks, stinks of indignation
and of wounded prayer, of a tongue undressing inside a dry
    mouth, of viper.

Yes, it stinks of viper slithering through rooms where dreams
    swell with blood and
dead people. It stinks.

Now I have to go.
I leave you alone with your whales
concocting syllables to the water below dementia's gleam.
I see you happy, Odysseus of the fields,
near the boys of summer and their stubble
racing off with the swooping eagle and the restless heron
on that solitary island.

I saw the last light slipping from your eyes.
Now, wherever I go, I know he returns
with the sun in his heart.

Until I die, he will always be beside me.

From Atlántica and the Rustic

Translated by Lara Crystal-Ornelas

> *Despite the blood he procures*
> — Lope de Vega

I

MY FRIEND IS FROM THE TRIBE of lone men.
He sees the sea. Looks at his silex belt, his dark amniotic sac.
He admires it.

He lives in the Arboretum of simple things. He knows
   the origin of the epidermic, the number of vertebras
   on serpents, the twisted stem of Sainfoins the
   incomprehensible shapes of buttercups. He always points
   out the capillary vertigo of the word *sea*.

He searches the maps for The Indies, their fresh poplars of
   ink.

His game is the whip that consoles him, it provokes him,
   it makes him spin, prophetic.

My friend sees the sea, burning in darkness,
its milk consumed, its lip ending with an eye.
His childhood, light lost among the legs of a spider,
a wound, open to piety. Bitter grass and ash.

His trade, fossil flower that makes him fall when he trembles,
   his heavy step toward us, kids, who don't know how to
   remember!

Brachial cell,
operculum? The sun, a gastric mouthful,
the moon, acid on its body?

My Friend describes the sea as proud and confident, a lustful
extension of a thousand feathers of elegy
with a thousand birds that recur, appear,
and always return.

His life: an organ on reserve, a fortuitous substance.
My Friend lies improvised, conserving himself.

One root forms through his beard, the sea grows on him and
    its cloud of smoke, its quick diving smile with a hundred
    bronze masks, abysmal.

He designates himself in the genus of *Felis.* Nettle, apiary,
    he calls himself generically: *Felis catus, Felis pardus, Felis
    tigris, Felis mar.*

His life begins with a measure of adventure, with the ultimate
    mistake of embryogenesis. He whistles and throws stones
    at the orchestra
of aquatic birds that bother him.

For my Friend the word *love* does not possess anatomy, he
    doesn't have any animal type. His body is corneal matter,
    calcareous, where he smooths the verb, he bundles up and
    begins a dream.

I dreamt, he told me, that there were flowers without whiteness,
    of one sole, open heart. Radiolaria, with their melancholic
    forms, poured the steadfast water over them, like a kind of
    nocturnal mouth in the freshness of their senses.

Dragonflies! The body, the symbiosis in knots of legumes.
Of plants—he thinks—nourishing mistletoe, humiculae.

My Friend now talks of microbes. Their eye, he says, is a
    vibration so luminous, that there is no ear in between,
    there is no oval window for a secret. I could be a Superior
    Member of that species, a ciliate.

He prepares a cure with a purple flower and an herb that
    resembles his testicles. He knows it will quench his ardor.

The rays of light are already burnt out. My Friend abandons the
    corpse, he embraces himself like a rooster to the flower stalk.
    He rubs his skin with his tongue.

At times, the profound is a speckle of light on his entrails.

My Friend is now in a divided limbo: he has a notch and a bite.
    He pronounces *the blood that takes*, its ventral syllables, its
    scales.

Animal for him, signifies a penumbra.
The spore of his thirst is the fire that crosses him.

His body is of the lone man.
His tribe, a larva.

III

VENUS WASHES HER GENITALS in the jungle. She
     purifies them.
Her purple gaze deceives the warning.
She drinks the potion of dry cola with fine honey seven times
and an ounce of saffron to fill her body.
It's the ascent.

He knows that in his stand of leeks and sunflowers,
the scream is a stubble that grows.

All the clarity in the filth that separates him from the wasp
     nest.
The subtle signs are what he doesn't confront.

The eye's potency is the extent of his force.
He gently places white cords beside some bulbs.

Iridescences. He remembers the formation of worms in the
     periphery. The substance set in the tree of life. And in
     front, the superior parabola: *abundantly.*

His freshness is of ripe wine, his scent of rocky hills. The
     suction cup is his longing, in cells of amazement the
     indigo is a page of glass. He takes note.

Alerted eye, visible, petiole. Everything for swimming is on
     the surface.

My Friend extends to the depths of the sea's clay in
    formation.
He happens to associate with the individual life. He goes with
    the worms,
bland symmetry of two points.

On the precipice, an ordeal of thistles falls apart at the
    bottom. His voice delirious. He strikes the battle of those
    who keep quiet. My Friend loves.
I know because he paints on laminates of uranium: *redivivus.*
He softly pronounces the name of the blackthorn, he has said
    that below the sea, the sands are very fresh and so porous.

Above there is a fence. We ascend through a path of dense
    scurf and rough slabs. Snakes.

The sun burns the herb in ash. He says, the adventure of rain
    is the alchemy of air. In its particles, I know that he loves.
My Friend sees the sea in his writing.

IV

DESPITE THE BLOOD HE PROCURES. He recounts.
He dries his herbs over *cracked* clay tiles.
He endures time diligently. No strength remains for the soul's
   age.

My Friend sees a bird of light in the window. Its chest. Its
   orifices. For
certain, it sustains in nature. It's an omen.

Barbarians, he says, lick their death in pure wine. There are
   rocks.
He cracks an egg in a glass of alcohol and drinks.
My friend is minimal.

The myths are solemn. His voice is thick. Prodigious voice
   in its warp.
Emitting vocal syllables.

The compass, he tells me, is to always walk along the
   vertebrae.
His grace is impalpable like the compassion of dreams.
He is the bird. After all, the beating of his wings always sways
   me to traceless places, to profane places. I follow his flight.

We arrive at the pastures together. There are red-haired cows.
An alligator licks my shadow in its harshness. There are tulips
   below a pear tree.

My friend concentrates. He dries sweat to the flight of
    canonic syllables.

The weight of water is guarded by a raspberry,
the rain a Sibila on Samia land?
Everything blossoms differently. My Friend tries the color
    of the raped.
The barbarians live six hours from here. They paint the lips
    of their sex with sulfur.
The forest thickens his diseased organs.

My Friend recollects his fondness of "an artificial sun."
Far from his beginning lives another bird who sings his
    ardor in our language. In the flower bed, a long viewed
    bromeliad stretches out its love in a hot horde. It's enough.
My Friend is the lover of simple things.

V

A PATH OF PERIWINKLES. There are no thickets.
My Friend names the sea that guards him. Here his syllables
    are cardinal points. He sees an islet of algae covered in
    gold where eagles cast out their hymns.

Appreciate, he says, the Sacred Family in low land. It's
    admirable that they preserve the taste of their hunger and
    thirst in filth.

I envy what has no end. His Arboretum. His virgin tongue
    that hollows out the alveoli.

The heart is superior if it protects the collecting flowers and
    the stupid beetles. He inflicts.

His call is from the leaves of the rose, exile where the birds'
    anger submerges.
My Friend shares his dwelling with parasites.
There are circumstances, he says, in which the safest point
    is shelter from the absurdity. Profligate, satisfied, he
    accumulates what separates: the masculine and the
    feminine in pallid seawater, reconciled.

The barbarians wash their eyes with vinegar. They bleed their
    teeth with alum.

My Friend covets misery. His shadow in flames.
He says the sea is a paintbrush for the page.

VII

CAPUDA. Escoletia. Raramis. Flumio.
He invents the black sun, the panic of flax, liquor's attire,
 argent. The medics ignore him.

He repeats: *Adimaca-lustis. Cypria-mantlix.*
Thinks of shameful things. The soul.

The edge of his name tortures him. He comforts himself in
 the crack of a rock. He sweats drool.

Movement is always a declension. 1/4 degree of latitude
 vivifies him, he breaks his ties to all things. What happens
 is not a vespertine figure, he says, and the Sun and Moon
 are the mast where he contemplates his opulence.

A faint, intoxicating bellow is heard in the larvary.
It's the arrival of widows, they've come to paint the friezes,
 the ridicule, a painted yellow bird. It wasn't always like
 this. Before, it was scarlet forked trees, the iodine base of
 the palms. The widows move about. They cover their soft
 rolls with cloth and cotton, remnants of a vain life. They
 lick each other's stretch-marks and devotedly defend their
 long scars, they drink water.

The row of aloes rest along the wall. They mark a river, a
 journey for the eye of the eagle.

Habit is the urge of his silence. Well, it doesn't mean a thing.

Below the lindens, sweet clover, salvia, the rasping danger of
   segregating a name—equivocal substance—and not being
   able to rectify it with the spit of that metropolis: a human
   city.

The sea, says My Friend, is far away so that we think of it.
Dream its lights.

VIII

I HAVE TO MAKE HISTORY and desire the dust.

There was an army of nettles and damiana covering the field,
a place of rubble where the rain made its delights: licked
crystalline bouquets. Grapes. We ate figs and grapefruits,
the snakes drank their milk beside us.

My Friend said: there's a difference.
What doesn't see its limit, remains.

Birds in flock, blighted vines, algae and rotifers at the point of
their purest ovation and the ephemera, in the web of their
similarity.

Life is simple because the day declines.

My Friend knows the happiness of his limpets' leaf. He loves
his innervations, its weak points. Below the ossuary, he
paints his inveterate History, at the foot of the wall, he
speaks of his battles. Without diameter, he repeats, his life
is only voluntary blood and water. Chlorophyll clouds
burn between his teeth.

He howls at night. He thinks of the wounded flesh of his
laminae.

My Friend is collective. Everything that was, doesn't fill the
world.

Life is immoral among the fig trees. Their leaves fall
  indissoluble.
Justice, calm.

The barbarians lacerate leaves, they smell of blood, they gnaw
  their margins with pig fat. They hang a sheep's heart below
  the myrtle.

My Friend decrees the ash. It's the ridicule. A heart more
  simple than custom.
My Friend dreams the sea in laminaries. His moist tongue.
His offerings.

IX

A BURNTLIME BULL BELLOWS in the summit.
When the sun reaches him, it opens his melancholic veins,
    tastes the heart of bivalves. The Center is the beginning.

What my Friend sees is a clamor beneath the night. Warm
    tiles shield the cross of the anchor, fish in geometry, date
    of arms on a point of the crisscross and that air that offends
    the dead god taking its harsh revelation.

My Friend thinks of tireless masses, virtue of the vain. The
    sentence of being one to one with the trunk.

In one year the Earth passes Saturn 57 times, He says. The
    bull resists. Haloes of fear and shame pierce him.

Oxidations of the skin form the wall.
Blood, a known energy? Its glands.

My Friend urinates slowly in the larvary.
The blood of mares infuses itself, raw, on the males.
The view of the bull dominates its head. It is necessary.
The world happens, it shakes, it disperses in an exact line.
Liquid of life. The bare bull, its exquisite cavern.
Black garlands under light softened by urine.

My Friend says: Life alone forms a labyrinth. We must choose
    to look into distance: the man-circle or the man-frog.

My Friend sings: life is an eyelash where the world shatters.
Where the world shatters.

XII

WHAT SUBVERTS. Like one who digs.

On the edge of the pulpit: celestial calligraphy, the focal
    point of the ambiguous. The Arboretum. He says a long
    phrase for his maps: *Clarisa, the Adorer, rubs her buttocks*
    with cyanide.

His numbers burn against the stinging nettle. Sacrificials.
And the horses grow impatient for their tears.
Who carves the shape of his face?
And the bats. And his future.

The mist is my only deviation. Take note.
Everything surprises in intervals. It's reflexive.

What doesn't change moves away from the safe haven.
    Opposing a point, he coordinates in amazement. The
    Order is built upon what it favors. He exhales.

There is always a ripe fruit in the tree. *Vice of men.*
    A multitude meticulously suspended in gold. *Vice of*
    men. Impossible incarnation. Longings are a passionate,
    ventral circle, the uses and habits of the genre, the spasm.
    Vice of men. Mouth with mouth, rapid, contour. *Vice*
    of men. Improvement is a provision that accumulates,
    a climate. *Vice of men.* The hollow segregates the
    experience, inheritance that drives confidence. *Vice of*
    men. The return organizes what doesn't grow. The ordinary

is inactive in existence. *Vice of men.* Well-being is a salient
point, what humiliates. *Vice of men.* Materiality deceives
cross-fertilization. *Vice of men.* The small always stay
behind, happiness of a symbol. Servitude. *Vice of men.*
Degradation has little room. Submits. *Vice of men.* Wise
implantation of will to fatigue. *Vice of men.* What's certain
is primogenial, imprudence penetrates what it excludes.
Vice of men. Vice of men. Vice of men.

XIII

REVERBERATES. Depends, to survive, on a point.
A point. Devotion in the void. Everything is maintaining a
    boundary on the tongue of vipers.

It was his caste. His disputes,
those of a glistening heart. Choir of shaved voices.
    Amphibians.

Imperfection, its womb of water filling the waste. He licks his
    volatile syllables on a soft palate.

Play the instrument of his scriptures, his dark mouth on stilt
    dwellings, his delirious lacquer, the reduced sea of his
    language. His eagle soul contrasts with the brutal hilt of
    talon. He drinks in honor of the forest. Its thickets.

The barbarians unleash their packs. The lukewarm milk
    of their bitches prevails in their rabid blood. And they
    secure it.

My Friend resists in the myocardium. He passes from the sign
    of Gemini to the white spots of scorpions. He falls. His
    teeth tear the skin off sheep. His lungs.
He says: what is from the heart is from the blood.
And he secures it.
In spite of delight, he separates his alum viscerae.
The Observation: most perfect repercussion in what shines.
    Flashes.

My Friend knows of acids. He digs a sulfuric well, renewing
    his virile parts. He undresses.

I will give Earth what belongs to her. Her prayers.

In a slow stream the first glimpse of sun. Pronounced
    innervations. Their foliar lamina extends into surface.

What follows germinates quickly.
He says: the agrarian sea, ah, the agricultural sea.

XIV

THE CLEANSING FISH ARE NOW FOR SALE. Their
organs are dried at the market, divination of a world that
phosphoresces impurity in a fit of anger displayed on
plastic tables.
His incisions.

The sea opens. It illuminates a point that favors the lethargic.
The hairs of the snout, liver, spine, all his virtue in our
melancholic eyes. Who approves what he conceals?

My Friend contemplates his kitchen. A field, undeserving
of loudspeakers that hang in the vertigo of his desolation.
And on shelves of blue mosaics, the jars that preserve his
sense of equity and justice. Grief of honor. Herbs dangling
from a stretch of rod, pieces of a domestic sea that scalds
men.

He thinks of tulips.
What is aware of its modesty, blushes.
He gathers part of his orchard in the intimate delation of a
dream:
all is all in the harmony of a vain ribbon.

My Friend extends a drop of blood on what he inserts.
The delight is confirming the nonexistent.

He opens his notebook. He sanctions the need of an open
    calyx.
Like one who bleeds.
Like one who screams and divides into a thousand equal
    parts,
the ultimate notion of being someone.

XIX

SYNTHESIS OF THE AQUIFER. Enduring light of simple
   things.
In the hard peace, like a porous ball, like a glass of water in
   the stoma, shadow of purity on the edge, leaf that grows
   green, precise point of my carelessness, hidden, illustrious
   tribe, obsessed virtue, penetrated sail traveling to its final
   summer it opens and designates itself: small preliminary
   surface.

That's the interior. He explains.
And I continue with the dread of seeing one lone body in the
   world. Worldly, I ask, a bud in the glass?

All of him enters the hollow vines of night, in the night of his
   swallowing. Barren night circulating in water, night sown
   over wineskins, unleashing his laughter, invoking his fruits,
   night ravine, night valley, sacred night of the goat fronds,
   frond in the jungle of his stupor. Night of beckoning, night
   of shadows without place and without daybreak, without a
   stable that protects the delicate beings, the pre-pubescents,
   those of small gains and short strokes, the frothy beings in
   the field, hirsute predators of his journey. And this fills the
   udder blackened by his tongue, disturbing the foul odor of
   his night fires.

But the sea, the sea roars in the great night of his larva.

From To Tell

Translated by Paul Hoover

Her horrendous voice, not her inner sorrow
—Góngora

A cry
a single cry
just a cry
to the open air
a cry of porpoise or dolphin
of incandescent fish by the water
a cry of the sea that breaks and repeats
that empties
and in the time of salt
says everywhere what it says
that swells
that glows
a cry
a single cry
just a cry
of the blue inconceivable sky
that repeats
that advances
that grazes among the algae
the fetid rumor of the brackish
a providential cry in the voice of air
an unsustainable rhythm
in the throat
A cry that knots itself
in symphonic circles of joy
A terrible cry

that announces the first death
that stands on precarious feet
and dismantles shadows and grumbling
A cry that must choose
for between the walls the liquid deepens

The wall as a cardinal point
an agonizing smile
in the punctual
sweetness
of the one who is drowning

A cry disbanded
in a garden with thickets
a dream of blue light for the birds
A cry that in itself
is the size of the sea
and lives at the center of rapture
and with each step it yields
to the delirium of a sponge
that inflates in sweat and gives glory
to the time of silent prayers
A cry is the caiman's vigil
the unleashed whip of an ant
the fan of yes the same immaculate
air of an inhospitable grudge
that bends
The cry that smells of salt

a wild beast dry
horny
in the dusky collapse
of your herd
The cry distilled from minutes
marks the world that is world forever
in an open moment where never
passes nothing and everything dissolves
hurling itself to the bottom

Nothingness is reason falling
finally it's emptiness
its bend in the road most refreshing
when the tree
is erected in delirium
in order to sing from its purgatory
its novice illusions
almost vertigo

A cry is sleepless in its dream
faded almost hoarse it stuns itself
like a crippled animal
the cry breathes sleep inside
its eyes and evokes a sacrifice
a dark joy in a spiral of weeping

The cry moans weeps wallows
glacial polygamous decrepit

sinking into flakes and scales
into mud
the cry sleeps alone
in the hollow of useless blindfolds
its intoxicated pallor
in its cadence and fatigue
it buzzes between the glasses and the cans
the remains are still ripe
and the sweet song
of the flies to vacancy

The cry is deeply in love
and sweet together with the soft souls
Rosa in order to tell it to Rose
is a corrupt luxury
a brief heart
that detracts
The cry is the insistence
on misery is the sharp bite of hunger
under the yoke of a sugar mill
a fire burning
among dogs and rats
is a shadow that crosses
the fetid waters of wonder
and it's the clamor of three nights
of the sickness of women, hens, and female deer
when the gods
lose their harmony and quickly
offer their shame to the twilight

The cry is air
air that only blossoms
in the half-light of funerals
The cry is the voice of the obsequies
a wafer in the pupils
which prays "Praise be to God
without God's silent cry
infinitely bitter and dry
and the newlywed God the round impostor
who belches who vomits who repeats
fragrant at the pit and doesn't say
not to purify the skin
devour candles and beautify
blind beneath the definitive sun
lethargic in the accounting
of a glass-beaded God summit
red-hot incredulous God
who doesn't ask for pardon
in the omen of dead birds."

a cry
a single cry
just a cry
it whips in lines
and looks dissolved
between the vertices of song
(sings among the captive petals
And don't forget me in the diaspora
sing sing deadly like an archangel

about about to shout his song)
The cry is erased
between the breasts that slander
sinks convenes seizes
becomes and is consumed
penetrates licks fits
in cartilage of fire
where it resides

The cry is just a number
a notch at the base of the wall
as meticulous
as a *tokonoma*
utmost swiftness of spirit
freezes the Cuban's print
bevels the aperture in the absurd
that dominates corners of the language
that exposes itself as a maelstrom
of all the whales in the sea
is an emaciated shell
adhering to the pale shadow
that crosses our sleep
The cry
is a mixture of sperm
and civil life
in living circumstances
a sign of those black fruits
where peace putrefies
streaked by oblivion

where their error is overheard
in a Parthenon of voices
and the air unfolded fornicates
voluptuously and never knows
of the children awakening
in endless tunnels
lost

The cry
roams the meadows climbs sandbanks
is hidden in the smallest grains of the sap
and splits into two branches
at the curb
of the public gardens
Its light is a wandering stage
where the bodies drink
unchangeable as
the dried blood of vultures
The cry becomes stained, expands
to a canvas painted in bleach
and to wet fish markets in the cracks
that drip their thirst in cathedrals
It calls between shingles and gutters
for the white popcorn of mercy
It doesn't exist
in the vaults that invoke
either groans or excrement
they pour out their prayer to beauty

The cry looks and turns nutritious
among the filaments
subtleties of stalagmites
Its opacity contains and glorifies
the scars of crazy widows
the plagues of corrupted young women
At the center it's gripped at the edge
A luminous crust between the slabs
At night the bodies whip it
they lick it like a cat at the touch
in its delirium in its crevices
the world opens in a color in passage
it flaps its wings in sheets of salt in its integrity
and among the porticos
it feels its furtive gifts
of the filthiest birds in the land
The cry of a flowing spring that overcomes time
soothing of the wrong man
As an insect
lands on the leavening
and gives voice to the rhizome of God
between the lips "die
with bags under your eyes by the name
where quicklime levies a tax
on your dead children"
The cry is only a cry
of silky smoothness where a theologian
lives morbidly in dirty rags in small rooms

Slowly it's known in the cloudy discharge
at random in broken windows
The cry is the pigment of an incantation
between the orchards and the fruit
of fervent prayer
Drop by drop it sings limitless
into a pit of sky-blue ineptitude
where it drinks the blood by sips
and swigs and names the food
of the executioner
Its bitterness is slow
with the dryness of a sponge
lifeless and scratchy
its devotion like a fever
(To Dimas it tasted like salt
in his bleeding
In Barabbas it was only a fruit
a swordfish in the balance
on the cross exhausted)

Humble and persistent the cry
it is always the acid that saturates us
in agony a single weeping that spills
in the slow endless afternoons of suicide

a cry
exceeds climbs sweats
when God tells us numbly

there are no nails no rituals
in the recurring tumors of the righteous
The sun burns your tongue microscopic
in the crack that robs us
dropwise prim and proper

There is a thirst that refreshes us in clouds
In the briefest cottons
of urgent slowness
There is a threadbare tethering
in the stillness of a tree
or in the piles of stones that wall us in
the blood in the waste land
if the cry grows in variety
profuse by the fire
fragrant crazed
from being the deaf hollows
that nest in men

The cry
opens its strength with a wedge
and falls silent grants light doesn't sing
where silence
is an openness of the spirit
Its spirit in self-controlled scales
is a source
symphonic in color
and the vertigo that rises in the corner

in which I am at the precipice
in the millimetric skimming
of the page

This is what I am and what I cry
that I am not boneless
given to babbling
a smooth speech
that which my blood speaks one before
one after the world and for the eyes
a warm animal that centers me
Wolves hyenas coyotes in my
heart inside the sumptuous
porphyry of blood
they gasp and they feed
on the warm flesh
that hastens the blood in me

Flesh of a cry I am
in proletarian forests
in indigent caves
where the vultures
in my voice defecate
centuries into the future
Meat asleep a cry
waiting on the shore
a convenient body
yellowed and rotten

so that it burns
so that it is
still
so that yet

a cry
a single cry
a cry scarcely measures
a metropolis
and refers
to the apostolic light that awaits
where never
nor no one
nor either

so that it speaks
so that it hears
its galaxy of dirty white stains
its sweet germination of clots and appendices
its drunkenness and such ecstatic weeping
that hosts and increases
its thirst on which it agonizes
and slows down in the arrogant
capital of merged lines
banished
Lightning by day
is the fury of the cry
if it goes clumsily jogging
on the ledge if confused

fragrant and so very semantic
where for you for me for everyone
trembling abdicates
its tin-plated trot
its rhythmic tension in every muscle
is a passing with no one on the horizon
riding as if nothing
ever departed or faded
for centuries unclear
for the fetal prairie of the deceased
where time nests among vipers
and agonized men redeem
the muffled hum of dreams
in the dream of being silent
its lying silence centuries of death

To cry or not to cry is the question
The stone that scarifies
and arises in only a face
in onyx borax flint
the triangular stone of an episcopal
silicate where the air crackles
the world of a slingshot
contained
in ulcers of shadows

The stone from the ruins that assays itself
where there once was a cry or outbreak
in the instant in which it envisions

the blinking blue of the disasters:
that time when we lost
the rage of children unburied
(The stone the cry the outbreak
the hour in which the night
is twice
brief)

At last the secular water reached me
it looked at me face to face with the stones
of a pool architectural and empty
where the cry lives in its
eager bloodless
anonymous monastery
its century of sinister
meetings
red-hot
stopped between my lips

From Nobody, the Eyes

Translated by Leticia Hernández-Linares

BIRDS

I

I have arrived at the night. A lamp illuminates me amidst the
grass.

Beneath a burdened sky the birds feed from the silence.

There are shadows of dust on this soil, why am I within its light?

II

I have seen caution fly like a graceful bird in the freshness of
age.

Above a bird remounts its flight and with the air's handwriting
shows me its fondness for the smallest trees.

III

It rains in the breath of dawn, in the country where the beast
roams like a human shadow.

I think about the vowels for the ascension of the light.

I hear the insect's purpose beneath the leaves of winter.

I see my mother's eyes in the flight of the birds.

She has died with the twilight in her heart.

IV

There was fire here in the impurity of a prayer.

Splendor remains of open gardens to the health of dahlias
and gardenias, to the brambles in the silence of sadness.

Our house will be tormented by that vision.

V

Morphine wears out in the sweetness. White sheets like the
clamor of beasts without compassion.

A bird pursues me through tunnels of shadows like an
immense melancholy.

VI

I feel the water, the mountain flower, the dust. There is ash
beneath the grass. I feel the lethargy of the water in the
rosebushes.

It rains on my mother's hands.

VII

The light is on the earth's bandages. There are cancers in the
harvest of sand. Lesions of mauve scars.

The exhale of the heavens like a single line on our hands.

VIII

The branches of my body remember you.

Ah, the melody of a rock on the mountain.

IX

The angels have arrived in cargo ships.

They are a ravenous pack in the place of profound fear.

X

I hear a bird in its abandon. A little girl in the sanctuary of the
    night, a young woman calls to apologize at the edges of the
    afternoon.

XI

I saw the heart of the wind in the tillage, the field in every
    burst of breeze,

your image in the coolness of the abyss.

Later, a royal courtyard where birds blaze under the realm of
    their song.

XII

Someone covers your body with silence. I spell out your rose
    garden in the perfume of your sadness.

XIII

There are large flowers in the depths. Solitary virgins at the
hour that your cry illuminates another place.

XIV

Sunshine at midnight. I have arrived at the emptiness. There
is a rough and silent flower in the sweetness of absence.

XV

The offering of salt is done by the north winds. The fire jumps
and spreads over every single one of the words, in every
single one of the silences.

I name you amid the creases of solitude.

XVI

I came for you from the dream beneath the blind grass. That
was happiness: that which had no reply.

Between your body and my hands: a lament.

XVII

I have arrived at the night and I am fearful. I have felt the
righteousness of sadness shelter under new grass.

I've seen the worms gnaw at my slavish condition.

Free me from loneliness, I'm freaking out!

VERTIGO

I

I come from vertigo, from the Holy Father's ether and I am in ecstasy.

I lost forgetfulness in the walls of silence. Like a slippery fly I traverse eternity, the hunger of regret.

II

There is a scar on your mother's injuries. There is a thorn at the midafternoon, a figure that grazes and touches the inflammation of what you see. There is a viper that crawls inside your throat with a song of light next to where night bleeds.

Someone licks your blood in the gallows.

III

Disease deafens in its brick. The sun penetrates with a ray of light through the air of your mouth. Shadows enter the bedrooms of the tides. They are the virtue and the opulence of one who agonizes with his secret among the hills.

Insufferable the thirst at the horizon of all the corners that inhabit you.

IV

There was too much shade on two occasions. I loved you
spinning in the darkness and the air shouted at you in the
vertigo of all the sweetness, in the footprints of an old god
who trampled on my pupils.

V

I have already known the hesitation. I yielded to the weakest
flesh, weak myself and worthless. I cooed the pulp of
invulnerability,

I was small and I was cold like a bird at the mercy of the disease.

VI

Your voice profanes a name in the emptiness.

The clouds flee like enormous butterflies in the night's bridal
flight.

My freedom nests in your servitude.

VII

I'm here next to your body. The birds peck at the rim of
imbecility,
"Leave me alone—" you would yell—"let me dream!"

You are the image of a woman somewhere else.

VIII

Cartilage backlighted. Clouds over the path of blood
and under a courtship of old idols a fly perches,
immaculate, and sinks into the impregnable.

ECSTASY

I

Snakes. They had traversed the yellow plants in the garden to
    drink the light haggard by the figure of certainty.

We saw them, excited, the way an intoxicated flower might
    appear.

II

Exuberances. Someone is in the fullness of the forest.

I savor the strong smell of vanilla like something that
    reconstitutes in my heart.

I feel a burning heat without the shade of the forests.

III

They cut down the trees in the middle of the afternoon.
    Green bolts of lightning left their scent in the weariness.

A slight bewilderment shines in the hint of the rose and
    gardenia.

We found out misery is beautiful if you forget it.

IV

It was said that there was always light on its forehead and that
a mineral spring flowed in the boredom of its evenings.

We yearned for reality in the vertigo of its sleeping quarters.

V

Something like a shudder appeared next to the night machines.

In silence we knew the recklessness beneath the eyelids of
abandonment.

VI

She smiles and a universe forms in her small mouth.

She talks of domestic things, but something eternal blossoms
in her breath.

The clarity startles her like an ancient sorrow.

VII

The grass grew dry amid the rubble. You rubbed your hands
on the slaughterer's table. The ducks showed their impurity
among the cranes hanging from the branches.

Ah, the clarity at the edge of decomposition.

VIII

A disquiet woke us from our childish dreams; the howl of the
 wolf lost in the profoundness of the day.

IX

Kiss all that destroys you: imprecision, vanity, incandescence.

Your purity is in the eagle's flight when it rises in search of its
 gods.

X

At daybreak a trench opened next to the library.

Its fantasy: to sow a swath of lilies.

The most profound serenity had arrived.

XI

The immutable is simply joy for your heart. Remember: you
 are no one under the still and quiet air.

XII

Clots burst in sleep. Buzzards convulse above. Flowers from a
 fountain brandish in the bellies of children in the night.

XIII

Commands to the heart: lick the dew of the blessing of the
    absent.

XIV

I see her dead like a diminutive particle on the dry grass. In
    the catamaran, I watch her look at the flight of infinite
    clouds. Her body, a bottle empty for many months.

SANITARIUM

There is a bird in the back of my eyes. (I missed all the
    reasons why.)

A whisper of rainfall and lightning, a clarity (I don't even
    remember the smell of the horseflies),

a mist of distant waters that reverberate inside my heart
    (I don't keep decadence to myself);

the clay in the geranium of your body. (I haven't been able to
    pretend: I love precision.) Hands, the trace of death and of
    desolation. (Now you pass by the mirrors, there is nobody
    there.)

I see a woman smolder like a madwoman abandoned by
    the birds. I see her body by the domes seething from
    forgetfulness.

The one that agonizes arrives. The eyes of the one who
    screams, a nothingness that germinates and opens like a
    long wound (what god submerged in the abyss awaits us?)
    The days

that get lost in the middle of the night (like subterranean
    drums)

where silence and living get confused (in a forest of blood)

where a heart of shadows dwells (the one that leaves prickly
    pears on your pillow)

with the omen and misery of the one that agonizes (a heart
    of birds in your water basins)

where the century with its fables doesn't reach (when the
    bulls bellow beneath the fig tree)

when nothing can be seen or judged, although quite near
    (and it is my delight)

I don't know who I can be (I lost all the faces, left all the
    names in the town of spilled guts);

now that I truly love the night and God licks the sweat from
    my eyelids (Christ doesn't know how to age)

and I am here calling you from the abyss,

but what am I doing inside of your eyes?

From Impossible Dwellings

Translated by Stephen Kessler

Aren't those impossible dwellings
perhaps your true properties,
earned inch by inch for the territories
of eternal goodness?
—Olga Orozco

What is that God
to be praised with all our sadness,
if not love
or at least the wonder
of being a body full of blood.
What is that
to be always the Nazarene
in that garden of furious
birds pecking your eyes out
in the pallid air.
And what about the pity
of the flower with that crystal
goblet spinning your body
in spiderwebs.
All of you aflame deliriously
burning like a triton
before the lure. How many
sighs sprang out of the ground
to say you came to throb
circling temples and markets
with your carved strength
in the slobber of the slaughterhouses.
Why did you shout

so many times into the clouds,
"I dare you!" and alone,
inch by inch,
you were afraid. And I rose
into the air and protected you
in this smoky genesis
the way all those years ago
I saw you with your burning
crown of writhing snakes
crying under the forked lightning.
Your shadow was the mist on my skin,
dawn's metallic prophecy. And you
were bleeding drunk
like a dry leaf slowly
falling, going mad.
Shelter me Lord in your barbed wire
and come up with me into nothingness.
Remember we're old
and plagued and we're blind
nocturnal angels
watching over sleeping
children
and the children
dawning
out of our dead
selves.

(for Álvaro Mutis)

IN THE PISTILS

I saw you born of light where the lineage
of a blood-red sun between clouds
pours its clear light into the roots' voices.
Entering into your dream I awaken,
shadows are dawning in your bedroom,
the world flares green in your name
where blazing fireflies are scattering.
From the heights of your harmony you bless me
and with your mouth's mud you form
a piece of me like your own history.
Within your tongue the breath is quieted,
the hoarse voice of your curses.
Your skin lifts me in its rhythm
and in the lines of your verse I hear you heavily
devouring my flesh and my ferment.
Everything in me advances then stops
and everything sinks into a sweet cry:
what I wasn't what I'm not,
what beclouds me and disappears me, animal
licking the afflicted animal.

What in the ocean holds her?

My stillness comes from the air
to look at you through this hand
as if the ocean were yours
and you were no one's.
From you I learned what it was to be
a single gust of wind,
a dark voice subtle before grace,
fragile within the forest's density.
Then I ran like an alligator to meet you
at dawn in the exile of an insect.
From water you taught me that miracle
where moaning in a fogbank
meant living all night long.
I still remember the river
of oranges and the parrots
chattering the announcement
of your first bedazzling.
Then you galloped into the pass
refreshed
by the cows' murmurs.
You were a child's heart against the wind.
And when the leaves fell,
from the bellflowers and the immortelles, immobile
under thunderclaps' swordplay,
you traced the trail of a command
with the barely contained fervor

and reverence for a place where a spell is cast.
And facing dawn's gargoyles
you saw in the distance
an irresistible sky
for falling body to body
into the streams of an island
under the shuddering of a spark
and that terrible goodbye
in the grass's ancestry.

What can save her from time and nothingness?

Then you came out of the night
when we were slicing hunger out of bread,
when fronds of blood
were driving men's destiny mad.
You sprang up into the wind and the clouds
when fire was flinging toward the rocks
the time when insomniacs are vegetating,
when mouth to mouth transparent
dreams were crackling like a balm
of shadows saying syllable by syllable
that night's names, the flash
of the deep rush. Then out of the sky
came birds, blind horses, and you,
captive in the confidence
of taking the first steps,
went out under the premise
of being one in the world and silent
next to the sun's thirst
on a glass page,
a single mirror, where we all saw
ourselves dying of astonishment.

IN THE PETALS

Your voice shoots out of the foam like a sacrilege,
secretly reducing me to drunken ash.
Your lips slide away from me into the world,
your tongue expanding, overwhelming, overflowing me.
The smell of your sweat is a song of light.
Your tongue is an avalanche where
life tumbles rumbling, wall
of the same wise god
who presides over his rivers
and branches of bloodstreams
and drunkenness
driven to naming.

The flowers' marriage opens atop the stigma.
Their pollen is scattered in the early dawn
and for a moment life is redeemed
and then withdraws.

The penitent saint cries
to let her greatness be her strength, dancing
in that unscrupulous realm. Teresa
is sovereign in her magnificence and with her birdlike
voice in its fullness warns: "I write
wide open with hyacinths
suddenly I know
I'm alive." And her language
tinged with so many mysteries, its brilliance
was that fertile framing
with her braids, her cheeks on fire
with hieroglyphs and with ecstasy
the pleased angels
licked the fear from her skinny body.
"Lord, what happened
happened, now move me to pleasure
and with your wings tell me who
will be for me that one reader
with self-enraptured heart
who'll fruitfully pray: Bitch,
let's make this world together."

What climbs her into the cloud-shrouded peaks
of thought and memory
and stands her gray facing the day's supplication?

And at the crest of all power
that dry night
among the festive branches of a church,
you launched a seed into the wind,
sinner of which temples,
to announce a soft smell of earth
arriving with sleep on its shoulders.
Where miner of the fields
were you light
or a light desire
indulged
and lilies sprouted from the stones,
and leaves from their sweet stems,
that dish of tender blood
for curing your scars,
for healing you anywhere
except in fear.

Your body like a beehive.
Where the ocean between your legs is held back.
Dead in life dead in dreams
your voice is the only root reaching out of a single shadow.
You are crucified in the cornfields,
in every nectar of the rocks.
Your ghost crosses the plain,
a sprig of lavender your hollow words.
Your hands sprout lightning,
its little sparks eat at your eyes.
Rain sweeps over slowly
and from its fear and its astonishment
two grieving butterflies emerge
and light on your gate.

What darkness runs from her like a doomed
and mythless queen and plunges her
into the day's writing?

You are the sea's daughter in your third
stranded syllable. Beautiful and prophetic
with your lance and an angel
lifting you into clouds infinite
in the distance. Chaste
you of the raised eyes, you cried
in secret beneath
the cross you worshipped, laughing
at the stuck-up moon with your long
hair undone. Blue
was the sound in flight
from faces and old predators,
when the animals
were mating with your
gown of a spilled virgin, skin turned
inside out in the stained glass now,
at night, draining your blood. Dressed
for battle, in that regiment
you're enlisted in, you ran
like a lucky lunatic, your golden flesh
glowing in sacrifice
to every gaze. Being
who has arrived or everything
forever far and flowing away
in the distance.

IN THE COROLLA

The vapors of your roots are in the sky.
Your gaze is of the water and the air,
you flower in the rain like a lotus
unleashed on the ocean from wave to wave.
Your tongue is on fire with the grace
of a child who's beautiful because dead.
You advance toward him through the flames
of a sun above his body where you emerge
beleaved in it in an embrace
flying out of the secret centuries.
God, you're saying, drinks light in the air
along the edges of the fragrant
nectar in the sugar mills.

What hieroglyph is she deciphering
in her sovereign prodigy
erasing her from dreams and from oblivion?

If you could be reborn from me
between my hands, under a cloud
of flies night after night,
for you the silence might be
the dirty old woman falling on her face,
the public under her skirt washing
your feet. Penitent like that, from coast
to coast under your tunic,
fear would call you
with a lightning bolt. If you called me
looking at what I'm seeing: the snakes
springing from your hands
and are a temple where you're screaming
visibly and invisibly in fields
lapping up praise, then
I might return to you being ashes
and outside a river of blood, a gloomy
Jordan layered in makeup, me fleeing
because of you in those waters, amphibious
in pity I'd show you
that net every time,
but quietly, I'd throw you into.

With just two or three stems male flowers explode.
They rise out of their own depths red hot and juicy.
They're knocked down by a free hand, they're raised
under this sky halfway between light and darkness.
They wither voicelessly and slowly die.

I might have been fast for him
riding a racing bike around the world. I would have
crossed even the classical
age in a blaze and extraordinary
above all in the period of eclipse
when the world was founded in an Acropolis.
I would have gone all the way to the first megalith
in its rigor and foundation and seen blue
that tender courtesan
sculpted in a quadrangle
vastly watching over it
from her lintel. I would have been
in a city of gold and ivory
in harmony traced in limestone
and an enormous slab of stone
in the shape of a pyramid, architectonic for him,
emphatic and captive between the gigantic
cliffs of a quarry. From East
to West on a racing bike I would have
ridden into that realm of birds
and serpents, through buildings and sanctuaries,
through inner doors and ordinary steps,

looking for him geometrical, an animal
making the facades more beautiful.
For him I might have been
a naturalist circling
that century testifying
to the New World between two wheels,
which not speaking but rolling
in their chains, carry me
into the breath
of an epic
that he, with all boldness
watches over.

IN THE STIGMA

A sword of light is what you curse.
At dawn jackals surround you
to invoke your moistening flesh.
In gardens of omens you tear yourself to pieces, your voice
is heard by the hallucinated fire
burning time abandoned to delirium.
I walked behind you driven mad
where the holy grasses flower.
For you the Lord's bitch rumbles
on the mountain, bends in the air
and is knocked down.

The old flowers received dawn's pollen
from the young ones, the way thirst
is undone by the first rain.

For you I don't pretend to be anything
but the fertile cloud of this coupling
the sacred vertigo where you gaze at me
looking at you from here like a she-wolf.
I can't let loose my demons
willing themselves into my smell
being one in the other being dark
in the divine guilt of this wedding night.
Pull me close to you subtly
and leave me to the darkness of this world
now all paralyzed because of you
and in first thoughts and last thoughts
turning to dust. Let my body's blood
be your blood, and the air
of my air be your breath. I love you
bloodily and with as much lucidity
as fireflies coming
and going in steamy madness
in the robbery of being chosen
for the pleasures of this I'm being
blessed with: hunger
in the hunger of completion
of being just an animal
passing through the world.

IN THE STALK

Because looking at you I have nothing even to call you.
I can't sing of you near the children in the churches.
I can't look at you out of another body or with the sail
between your lips and my cadenzas.

I can't bleed you like sap
or like the resins in the reliefs
that crave you like sea spray.
I can't squeeze you like thick lips
nor wrap you in my smell and my caresses.
Because looking at you I have nothing nor am I you.

You'll never see the ocean stripped
of her breath, exalted
in an eagle's feathers
glorious with that vertigo
that guards the thirst of making love
in grandeur. You'll never
have the real sky to see her
the same as the water's
divine nothingness. You won't be a shepherd
in the waves of her arteries
thrusting into the air her beauty's
imperial staff. You won't glimpse the sun
in the thunder nor the salt
in the laughter of her grace, it doesn't matter
if you curse every crest, you'll never
have the terrifying light of her spray
to gaze into her face to face with life.
You'll be forever birthed coming
out of her night, weathered with the sand
of her dazzling. You'll be
no one if you don't sing to her
like the white theological
birds of so many temples.
And though your tongue may remain
a rough-voiced animal, you'll
navigate from Pluto
to Mercury, a man
or woman adrift
on that ocean, concubine
to whoever's breath that is.

From If We Have Lost Our Oldest Tales

Translated by Lorna Shaughnessy

Night breaks free from its moorings,
raising the anchors of time,
and like a small boat lurching
strains against the swelling tide.

> We came from beyond the sands,
> walking the word paths,
> the path whose name is hidden
> behind the lids of closed eyes.

Cast adrift across the lake of thinking
where muddied giants celebrate
the rite of the sleeper.

> We crossed the sea as strangers do,
> and coming to an empty harbor
> surrendered our disbelief when we saw
> "three gannets, a river-bird like a pelican
> and the streaming tail of the tropicbird."
> We were wedded to their piping song
> and the droning voices that rose with the dust.
> Vestal virgins in the ceremony of the castaways,
> ritually dressed in precious stones
> and scales
> on the eve of departure.

Ever-burning stars,
divine creatures of the deep
lie prostrate in the spent sleep of the shallows.
The smell of their decay overwhelms us . . .

We have seen the sea cover its skin
with flowers from the dockside
like a blazing coffin in the midday sun.
But at night,
when the great tuna leap
high enough to touch their God
and the fish heralds miraculous events,
with our own eyes we have seen our dreams
shed their plumage,
untie their blue-black hair
and lay their bones to the young waters.
And on the beach,
where the crab,
like an insatiable priest,
sacrifices another victim
and the drunken coral wallows in its good fortune,
we listen to the brittle silence
undress the rain's rent voice
as our dream-feathers rise
in flurried tribute to the sun
who visits us each morning,
                    fleeting
as a secret lover,

and carries the sound of our moans
up to the top of the hill of portents.
One day in the sea, the next
in the glaring void of the city,
he is the one who
"hastens us to look into each other's eyes,"
hot, red-rimmed,
but defenseless
before our oldest stars, begetters
of lightning bolts.

Esteemed Trojans, fugitives
from the walls of burning infantry.
Where is the moon now, where the ancient cities
paved with prophecy?
Where is Hermaphroditis, the first fate?
Where is Cassandra's uncombed hair?

> We crossed the sea as strangers do.
> We dreamed, sleeping in the depths of those eyes,
> of the immeasurable vastness
> of valleys blessed by the tongues of cows.
> All the life of the shrines
> that towered in the legend
> of merciful trees.
> We dreamed,
> unable to tear our closed lids from the spray,
> or the soaring, soothsaying wind
> that blows through the city of the deep.

Where are we to look for life?
Where?
If we have lost our oldest tales . . .

We were not the women who died
beneath the homily of a faded rainbow,
homeless sleepwalkers
in the trinket-sellers' market.
Neither were we the mestiza daughters
of vulgar lies, spellbound
by the blue-handed wizard.
Nor the sluttishly dressed dolls
in dockside bedrooms.
Nor those joyless women from distant shores
with tears tattooed on their cheeks,
now buried in a plot with memory
and nostalgia.
We never strayed into the hellish docks
of the lost sailor,
never saw the sad miracle of stained glass
in damp cathedrals.
But at night, at night,
when laughter is forged from solitude
and all the forgotten images
of a sea that opens its jaws and roars
resonate in the mysterious rhythm of a heavy swell
that conjures a fabled land with its clamor,
we were there in the night,

fresh
to the agonies of time,
frail
and proud as a she-cat,
virgins
from large families,
madwomen
who rise naked at midnight
to tame
a burning bed of vipers,
and then,
tenderly,
offer them the white water of their breasts.
Our dream was the dream of mariners.

Night breaks loose from its moorings
and sets sail.
left behind is a palace
with empty courtyards and columns,
where the mad girl's daughters surround her.

We dreamed, and from a distance
heard a dead tongue speak to us:
I am no more and no less
than the infinite, deep abyss
where the wind hurls its sermons.
Shut away in my blindman's work
like a tropical disease,

slowly dying on
sepulchred shores.
Look, here I am, home of the gulls,
beating against dispossessed mountains,
the sites of apparitions.
and here again in the rush and clamor
of a neighboring port,
beside an altar of smoking stones
covered in mementos of a thousand wounds.
I am the one who bore the Ark of the Covenant.
The golden robe of the chosen few
was placed on my shoulders,
painted the color of orchids.
I was the painting echo
of another's lover,
the sentence passed down that set you
apart from the living,
the weightless orb of life
in your divining mirror.
I am the one who has always waited,
as certain as black stone
in dead places.
The one they paint in jade and silver
on urns and vessels
of the finest porcelain.
From above, where the birds fly,
the women who come here
seem to wear immense hats.

And the children,
who know more of me
beneath their closed eyelids,
build castles out of salt,
cups filled with paradise and ashes
where the castaway drinks his solitude.
Look at me! In the pained eyes
of that young girl,
in the old fishwife's laugh,
taunting us
with the secret she keeps behind her curling lip,
or hidden behind the ample skirts
of the woman who works the land,
plump and hoarse,
the solitary queen of the cornfields.
And at the table covered in a cloth of rain,
I am the ever-present wailing of the drowned.

Ah, clairvoyant slave
who climbed into the victor's bed
and understands the ways of the stars and the birds,
who sees the heavens' signs
shine forth from the caked sand.
Wife with a child's eyes
who slowly walks alone
through a forest of tall columns
erected in dreams.
A woman who calls out to the sea, her body

opens to the endless night, seething in anticipation,
while the sea, all hot craving,
rises up with a deep moan
to meet its final destiny.
Where are we to look for life?
Where?
If we have lost our oldest tales . . .

But there, above the waters
like a shimmering mirage,
we saw a city sculpted in the empty air,
and our astonished eye met
a smiling, invisible sun.

The castaways reach the highest peaks
and cross liquid plains to meet the dawn
beneath a gracefully arching sky, delightful
to the eyes of all who behold it.
The nameless ones.
The ones with salt in their blood
who put aside their childhood like songbirds,
cast a dawn lament out on the waters:
"How many more waves to make us weary.
How wide a sea must we still cross?"
And from the clouds that cloaked the land
came a band of pious women
crooning their sad, tired songs
with the cold comfort of medicinal herbs.

Suddenly we were halted by
the perfume of fennel, juniper,
and sweet yellow clover,
between the mountains and plains,
drenched by a dazzling cloudburst
of legends.

Beautiful
as dolphins in the Carpathians,
or black roses
in the hands of a fugitive from Asia,
they slept
as we sailed forth
on the Ark.
"The winds were light and perfumed."
"Give thanks to Almighty God,"
and from the farthest shore
they were dragged
ceremoniously
from sailors' lost nets,
screaming
in the all-engulfing darkness,
in the outpouring of purged images,
crying out in horror
to the stones that would build cold,
secret walls
at the very apex of their pain;
they were dragged

to new lands, made mad
for the love of lichens and ferns.
a world of fulsome green days
lit by a sun as old as time.
Like a clay-colored cloth the land
folded, and in its hidden creases
solitary birds built their nests.
Its beaches were long tresses of curling hair
where pale lamps brought ashore
the perfumed bodies of drowned women.

Ah, yes, it was you we chose from the depths
of sorrow.
when our faces, fresh
as the enduring essence of the
walnut's oil,
were stained a new color,
and the remains of that night
were branded on our bodies
with the purple of fig-skin.
Yes, we chose you at the point of entry to harbors
where the youngest of women
dream
of the wild ducks' journeys
to the Antarctic.
We chose you at the river-mouth,
the launching-place of legends and tales
that seek higher waves.

We chose you above all the sails
that cross the wide kingdom of the winds,
while the heron's cry
opens like a wound,
a final flourish on the water.
"Yes, you are the chosen one,
with you I will make my covenant."

Where are we to look for life?
Where?
If all that remains are the perfumed bodies of the drowned . . .

We thought, brushing salt from scraps of seaweed,
underwater blood from the bodies of the
    shipwrecked,
about the lotions and perfumes that thrill
the body beneath its clothes;
about the many flavors of town squares
grown vain with the color of fruit stalls
and the flaunting of precious jewels.
We thought
about the pool of ruined words that lies
at the foot of the tale of tall mountains.
Exhausted at the sight of the ends of the earth
we traveled every path
that led to a madhouse.
There, on long wooden benches,
our birthright bled away in our

daughters' memories. We were mothers
to the human dross that gapes, awestruck,
at birds of ill omen and eagles
as they descend
from city to city
in search of human misery and hunger.
The sea lapped at our wombs of stone.
There were premonitions of that coupling
with the seas,
in the ever-branching corals
and the way the night moved
across the beaches.
We grew old,
and our bodies,
released from all clarity,
were embalmed with mud dredged from the depths.

Night sails on the deepest of seas
"A mighty swell cavorted in monstrous forms,
sending far and wide its bitter spray."
Time darkens. The storm retreats,
and the sun,
from its distant refuge,
licks the earth's brow of limestone and obsidian."

We died at sea level,
to the heart-rending cry of the black frigatebird,
the crimson torment of swordfish

and fish with golden scales,
mouthing the same Salve Regina
the sailors recited
on their watery beds.
We died,
and the moon slowly emerged
from behind the palm trees,
rising up to reign over those bodies,
as green as olive and nopal.
Like a nymph,
radiant in the low tide,
where oarsmen sank their offerings
as deep as love itself.

In the lone voice of the sea
a murmuring song rose from the depths.
The wind told tales of great deeds
from beyond the sands.
Trees sprang from the earth,
and from the trees,
the green blood of battles.

And we women,
still so far from the mountains,
going steadily mad
with the pounding of waves.
Voyagers with no end to our memory,
listening to the seaweed's blasphemies,

the perch's weary round in the small cove.
Our only consolation
the abandoned constellation
of silence

Hosanna, hosanna,
blessed be the Lord of our dreams.

Beggar-women from the regions of salt and spray
looked for something pure over water and land;
in the smell of dry leaves and cool grasses;
above the skeletons of gulls
and the purple mantles of mulberry trees,
in shrines and sacred sites
to the virgins of the sea;
in the jangling rhythm of earrings,
of bangles and charms dangling from wrists;
in the smell of violets and azaleas
and the legendary quickness of the hand that embroiders love
on its sheets;
in the dream-filled eyes of prophetesses
and the old healer-women's secret touch.
Women
who hold the ramparts and sacred places,
commanding trenches, aspersoria,
censers, ceremonial urns,
each and every thing devised under the reign of time.

It was the age of Orion
and they were our men:
kings of pastures and princes of herds;
valiant knights of the order of the jaguar
and knights of the order of the eagle;
powerful lords of battlefields,
governors over entire peoples
and insect nations,
ghostly astronomers who paid homage
to strangers,
navigators of angry waves
who offered up their lives to hope;
men who never hear the goodbyes that claim them
as they sail out from harbors;
men who wear the name of victory;
hungry men made of clay, both vessel
and mold.
Men
with their shadowy chariots,
with their blood-rites,
in the deepest unremembering abyss.
Our men.
They chose water lilies, lotus flowers,
Night-blooming Victoria lilies and crowfoot.
Voyagers lost in legend!
They learned about the limestone balconies
painted red for the slaves of reason;
the floors of cedar and holm oak

laid in libraries;
and long passageways
in the compassion of commandments.

Lights,
the glitter of shattered diadems.
Explosions that leave unmoved
the resting waters.

With a music that comes from inside;
with foul tongues that read
heavenly portents from afar,
with the lulling rhythm of swaying palm trees,
we sang of death: our lesser queen.
Watched by people of the peninsula
and the fishes in their little coves,
standing before a city's grave,
we sang of the many shapes of our desire,
listening for dreams foretold,
the sibyl's voice,
the mirrors' splendor;
for the laws of the tides
and presentiments of time;
for the breeze of bugle-call
and the burning scrub of war.
We sang
with empty hands and a stranger's tongue,
on benches, street corners, and in bedrooms,

in the scent of oleander,
the pure song of poetry.

Like a celestial chronicle,
their voice was carried up
and up to the top of the reefs.

Sailor,
sing a song from the rocky
coasts of time, the promise
that once again we will hear
the siren's voice.
Sailor who returned in vain
to home ports,
whose story flashes in a lighthouse beam
in dead valleys
that echo with the shrill cries of the departed
and long days that feed
the pelican's unhurried gait.
Sailor of the night
who grieves to see a seagull die.
Sailor with no soul but the daily,
rhythmic pounding of the waves.
Always moving,
inhaling
the salty aroma of oceans,
headlands, islands,
of children lost and the woman

who waits, resplendent, in the distance.
Sailor,
your song is the errant path of the winds.

And the first day of dawn brought wind,
and the children, decked out in their delight,
sang the praises of dry desert tracks
where a blind old man
foretold their destinies.

From every corner of the earth,
from the most distant and vast lands,
from lost places and in barbarous tongues,
from borderlands and kingdoms,
from flowering fields,
cornfields and the homelands of the nopal,
the golden meadows of Huexotzinco
and mountains black as sapote fruit,
from mysterious regions of flowers
and maguey agaves,
and from that place where the eagle's cry
resounds within the waters,
children will rise up,
inflamed
by the sea's arrogance.

"We come only to sleep
we come only to dream:

It is not true, not true
that we come to live in this land!"

> Alone, naked and in silence, they came
> through the very nerves of the city, carrying
> a garland offering
> of golden flowers. They followed
> the sound of the sea, walking
> with a shepherd's footstep, telling
> tales of the thunder's deeds
> and of great swirling winds. They were
> an army of stars
> in the depths of the skies.
> Glory, glory be to the migrant
> children who await
> the voice from on high!
> And to the sound of laughter and rapturous seas
> they blessed the forests, the town square,
> and the highest rocks in the abyss.

The wind prods an impassive sky,
whipping up prophecies.

> The sun beats down on battlefields.
> Children burn.
> Forget yourselves—commands the wind—
> sing of life as you face death.

Spurred on by the blood of exile,
by the slow syllables still shining in their hair,
they trace a horizon,
dream up a firmament.
Their dream, the waters of the sea.

From The Garden of Enchantments

Translated by Aurelia Cortés Peyron and
María Richardson

To me was all in all. — I cannot paint
What then I was.
—William Wordsworth

I

They all came from the sea,
with the glimmer of faraway faces,
always considered the loveliest.
Those faces wandered such lost dreams
made from a hard substance
that the house alchemists,
below a clear sun,
in burning sea,
transformed.
Resting on green stones,
we saw the terse and luminous bodies
that only the women
could wash to our amazement.
They spoke of the sea in great phrases:
of its salt skin and white feathers
where the ships slumbered;
of the penance that mother's lay,
with poplin dresses,
as seaweed bridges
for their daughters' vulvas.
They spoke of the shores
while the old ones set up great altars
and the dogs blessed the salt with their barking.

That world grew beyond the pale sky
listless to the sound of the bell
that sunk us into long vigils.
Long as lightning, like the straight hair
of those girls who tied it with a string of water.

It was a wave of people
that came and went
carrying the daze of that house.
There, before sunrise,
when gestures are bland
and sad in solitude,
I undressed and enjoyed being that way, happy
in the disorder of that land
so far from the sea,
yet so close,
with its nest of murderous birds
and its crying trees. Immense to the eyes
where a fish splashes between my games
and officiates in silence in the pond
of a never-forgotten region.
And the church claimed it was Lent.
The purple and gray time of ash:
song of fire in the room of the dead.
That bell of endless sound
still tolls in my head,
like a now old psalm
I keep among my ruins.

And it was morning when the sun opened its mouth:
　　　　—Look!—it said, and I saw how a lonely man
extended his white wings, like an ornate bird
that overflew the gardens of the house.
As he passed, the women bowed toward the field
　　　　—Goodbye!—they yelled. Then, like shrouded
　　　　　bitches,
they drowned their voice in prayers.
In their brick terraces I saw the old ones
consume their nights in the saltpeter
of ancient bodies and braid the wind with their hair.
I grew up where time lasted,
where the ragged dream
shone
poisoned by the stench of scapulars.
A dream dreamed below clear skies
in fits of laughter
between blue walls crossed by imps
that knew wonderful stories
and whistled the night away
in that cauldron of prayers.
But a creak was enough
in that pigsty of beautiful legends,
in that urinal where our life was diluted.
The softest noise
on the wooden planks
was enough
for the sea

to awake with the dead face
of faraway things.

> *A hill touches an angel. Out of a saint's cell*
> *The nightbird lauds through nunneries*
>   *and domes of leaves.*
> —Dylan Thomas

III

I was a girl then,
and sitting at the wind's gate
I opened the green night of trees,
the night of the lines of my hand.
On the other side, we slept in the darkest
areas of our thoughts.
We lived between weeded walls, panting,
our mouths gnawed by laughter
and names tattooed on our tongue,
when it was always too late
to run any further.
Do you remember?
It was the year after the Easter party:
there was a table with white tablecloth and at the end
someone spoke.
Then we bathed in the garden fountain.
We subjected ourselves to that chant each afternoon,
each time sweatier, more ridiculous:
limiting ourselves to smile.

Thus, sometimes,
when the sun disputed the dreams
woven of great stories,
our eyes were wide
and our stares long . . .
Then came laughter:
the legend of certain plants,
the devotion to touch,
the stink of lemongrass.
And then,
something of yours and mine
pounding us on the lips,
something that didn't escape
the garden's weeds,
something sacred
like the wind's complaint,
like the years stitched in winter parties.
And the women spoke of bird shit
at the basins of the dream,
like switching signs in the sky.
With soft words and slow lips
they spoke
of the names of our trees,
of the polished wood
where the steps of a dead child echoed.
Born next to the night
from the sea's purest womb.
They, like a long landscape,

open to the sea's hands,
the sea that rises
at the precise distance of the sky.
facing the wind,
and dressed with children's roars,
while they,
the old priestesses of childhood,
starch the noises of the house.
Ah! I remember
the first signs of the eucalyptus trees,
the persistence of moss,
the vast ignorance that descends
through the sticks of dead seasons.
I remember a piece of land,
no name and no title,
a lonely land,
fenced by the rain's patter
and I watered your flowers
while a woman aborted in the waiting room.
Then her scream, her clothes
spread out through the patio
like the color of roses,
the hair undone,
the body naked to the bone.
And the night shaken at the height of the tree
passed like a bird in a mysterious adventure.
We, then, sprung from the dream
half-opening eyelid shades;
to delve into you and me

the way you enter an ocean.
Ah! The world became an old ship
that departed from the skin's horizon
and crossed clumsy and slow
through the routes of my body.
You and I sailed full of sun,
with the salt of seas in our blood.
We were the heroes of the waves!
And from the height of the sky's fleet
we painted the sea with our eyes.

The wind set anchor in our mouths;
it smiled.
I, brother, listen to the tales of the fish
the way you listen to the wail of a dead brother.
I thought, then, that I was big,
and as such
I saw the old stretch out
in the shadow of the days,
through your eyes flowed that dark afternoon
in which you took in your hands
my childhood dream.
I waited
humming a song with closed eyes,
the moment to lay out, for you, a prayer mat
woven with the skin of my desires.
That afternoon
I saw you as a child,
I saw you infinite,

like that red kite,
whistling bird,
that you flew on cool afternoons.
You were the lord of the heights!
You, my brother, like a wisp of sun,
have made yourself heard everywhere.
And I, who was then a child,
sat at the wind's gate
to listen to that bird,
the way you listen to a dream
long forgotten.

VIII

At noon
a woman
washes her eyes
at a dream's limit.

Never did the earth see such sweetness in a face.

IX

You hear
the water spring again
in the earth's breath,
in a warm and strong voice
and the laughter, you still remember,
of the cloud, light and free,
as it crosses the water.

You contemplate
the garnished summit of the forests,
heightened by the light
of morning. Joyous,
you ran saying a name
that was cooler than the brick!
The day gushed behind you
and a sun of huge, transparent hay
nested on the palm trees.
How big you were here!
Beside the sick woman's children.
Beside the aromatic herb bed.
Ah! This green time
of golden fruit was the world's limit.

(Living below a thatched roof is enough,
in the harmony of stones that whistle
as they roll down the hill.)

Girl,
we'd have to see why the moon
gets lost between the trees and leaves you,
generously,
halfway through the fable. There,
lost in the peace of the gardens,
like at the Jabal pavilions,
the men trace
water's intimacy.
Beyond the hills

they rise jubilant
and play their conch announcing
the arrival of another day!
The sun,
in its lust,
ignites the cheeks of those perfumed
with warm water and the fragrance
of a *madame* anointed with linseed and castor oil.
The white plaza shines; the beasts,
tied below the green shade of an old tree,
rinse the dream at the troughs.
The feet, then,
travel a river of words
between the light of absolved images
in your eyes.
Apparitions embodied in pollen!
Flowers open to the day's resurrection!
Hail lady of the rain
and grace!
Hail the multitude of wives and emissaries
that nest in the mouth of lightning!
For theirs will be the kingdom
of the hills, the valleys, the abandoned
monasteries that dream of coral salts.
You hear
the earth spring again
in the water's breath.
The cloud shudders in the county,

and its rags,
like a vain word uttered by men
treated with gentian violet, make you think of enemas
on virgin mares and the fishing line
that always returns in the same anchorage.
You contemplate
the faces of the blind, the eyes of the dead woman
and her chest
scattered in the rooms of the house.
You sing
and your song gives birth to berries for men
of another Fatherland. And you rub
the heads of children
with a sponge moistened in coral paste.
Perhaps the earth lives on open water,
in the fecundity of abortions
or the white lead of paper.
Perhaps you
who dream of the fish charmer know
the glory of soldiers and cranes.
Perhaps you
hear the water spring again.

XI

An October sea
on the steadfast planks of the pier. A sun,
accustomed to the colors,
sleeps faded on the water. Suddenly my eyes glimpse

the darkened shadow of some hill.
It's a bad omen to see the poppy's stem.
Why are we so far away? The trees
have bequeathed their leaves to weeds. The men
passed yesterday with the wind.
They elicited long discussions below the noise of the storm.
And someone, between poultices and yeast,
begs,
with that sweet voice of the ill,
for a little bit of sea.
Wild mignonette grows on the outskirts.
At the shaman's place,
the men wear their fear in the open,
at night
they show their eyes still reddened by desire.
There are birds that seek crumbs on the table
and the women,
high sentries,
prophesy flight
with their masks of silence.

XIII

They all came from the sea.
We keep their silence between us.

Begetters of the first word
they were brought by the first grandmother:

"Sing in the White Mansion of the Sea
a brief, sour, and smelly song,
a faraway song
that will make us weep."

Lit by our fever's dream, they
move forward like the glint of an immense mountain range.
They laugh,
adorned with the blood of noon,
awaiting the arrival of the Sea Bird.
We keep their silence between us.
Charmers of the first shadow
they walk dazzled through the earth-born seas.

"We will only guard our way."

In the patio of red flowers,
the sound of a strange and rushed soul.

(Your hand returns to me,
your white queen hand.)
The wind women left with the water.

We keep their silence with the sea
that rises in our dreams.

CREDITS

The Spanish poems that are translated in this volume appeared in the collections listed below, all © María Baranda. English translations © Yale University unless noted otherwise.

Un hervidero de pájaros marinos (Ediciones Atrasalante, 2015)

Yegua nocturna corriendo en un prado de luz absoluta (Universidad Nacional Autónoma de México y Ediciones sin Nombre, 2013), translated to English by Paul Hoover as *Nightmare Running on a Meadow of Absolute Light* © Shearsman Books 2017. Reprinted with permission.

Arcadia (Ediciones Monte Carmelo, 2009)

Ficticia (Calamus Poesía, 2006), translated to English by Joshua Edwards under the same title (Shearsman Books, 2010) © Joshua Edwards. Reprinted with permission.

Ávido mundo (Ediciones sin Nombre, 2005/Cuadrivio, 2015)

Dylan y las ballenas (Editorial Joaquín Moritz, 2003)

Atlántica y el Rústico (Fondo de Cultura Económica, 2002). English translation © Lara Crystal-Ornelas.

Narrar (Ediciones sin Nombre, 2001), translated by Paul Hoover as "To Tell," first poem in *Nightmare Running on a Meadow of Absolute Light* © Shearsman Books 2017. Reprinted with permission.

Nadie, los ojos (Conaculta, Práctica Mortal, 1999)

Moradas imposibles (Ediciones sin Nombre, 1997)

Fábula de los perdidos (Ediciones del Equilibrista, 1990), translated to English by Lorna Shaughnessy as *If We Have Lost Our Oldest Tales* (Arlen House, 2006) © Lorna Shaughnessy. Reprinted with permission.

El jardín de los encantamientos (Universidad Autónoma Metropolitana, 1989)

Born in 1962, the Mexican poet MARÍA BARANDA is a winner of major literary awards in Mexico, the Aguascalientes National Poetry Prize and the Efraín Huerta National Poetry Prize, as well as Spain's Francisco de Quevedo Prize for Ibero-American Poetry. In 2018, she received the Ramón López Velarde International Poetry Prize, award for her career. Her many books include *Narrar*, *Atlántica y el Rústico*, *Dylan y los ballenas*, *Ávido mundo*, *Ficticia*, *Arcadia*, *Un Hervidero de pájaros marinos*, and *Teoría de las niñas*.

PAUL HOOVER is the author of the poetry volumes *The Book of Unnamed Things*, *Desolation: Souvenir*, *Sonnet 56*, *Edge and Fold*, *Poems in Spanish*, and *O, and Green: New and Selected Poems*. He is editor of *Postmodern American Poetry: A Norton Anthology* and the annual literary magazine *New American Writing*. His works of translation include *Selected Poems of Friedrich Hölderlin* (with Maxine Chernoff) and *The Complete Poems of San Juan de la Cruz* (with María Baranda). He teaches creative writing at San Francisco State University.